**Using Information Technology
in Businesss**

Maureen Mac

**Using Information Technology
in Businesss**

Using Information Technology in Business

Elizabeth Rae

PITMAN PUBLISHING
128 Long Acre, London WC2E 9AN

A Division of Longman Group UK Limited

© E Rae 1991

First published in Great Britain 1991

British Library Cataloguing in Publication Data
Rae, Elizabeth
  Using Information technology
  in business.
  I. Title
  658.400285

  ISBN 0-273-03726-9

Printed in Great Britain

Contents

Acknowledgements

I would like to thank Sandra Carruthers for producing the desk top publishing exercises and for all her hard work on this section of the book.

Guidance notes for tutors

The exercises contained in this book have been designed specifically for individual units of study and are student centred throughout, requiring little exposition by the tutor. This material is, therefore, also suitable for use in an Open Learning environment where students require practice material which will enable them to attempt internal/external assessments thereafter.

The material has been presented to meet the requirements of SCOTVEC Higher National Unit No 6400220 Using Information Technology in Business, but it is also suitable for SCOTVEC Computer Applications modular courses in Spreadsheet, Database and Word Processing, and for RSA, PEI and LCCI courses.

Although a working knowledge of computers is advised for entry to the HN Unit, it was thought necessary to commence each section with a basic, introductory level set of exercises in order that students might refresh their working knowledge of the programs prior to tackling the more complex tasks. It may also be the case that, although students have used computer programs previously, they are not familiar with the particular program being used for this area of study and this 'back-to-basics' approach should assist them in achieving their goal.

The exercises have not been designed for particular application programs, and the solutions have been produced using a variety of well-known software programs to test their effectiveness. The solutions should be interpreted as merely suggestions and the author acknowledges that there are various correct methods of producing and presenting material. However, sample solutions assist both the classroom teacher and student when interpreting instructions in new material.

The book introduces commands gradually and carefully, each exercise containing consolidation of those commands previously used. It is recommended that the exercises be undertaken in order. However, because the book has been designed to facilitate mixed ability teaching, it is possible to adopt a flexible approach with this material. The material has been divided into four sections to enable students and teachers to select the appropriate set of exercises. A useful guide to these is the Summary of Commands at the commencement of each section. Use of reference manuals or information sheets should be encouraged throughout.

Colleges may wish to produce their own set of assessments to meet the specific requirements of this Unit. However, an assessment assignment has been included in this book. This assignment may usefully be employed as a practice exercise to be undertaken prior to assessment. A thematic approach has been adopted to this assignment in order to give it a sense of realism and so that students may see their particular area of application study in context.

Guidance notes for students

If the thought of using a computer program, never mind understanding one, terrifies you, then you can count yourself amongst the majority. Most people have started off their computer training with reservations but, if you were to ask them now, I'm sure they would say they prefer working with computerised equipment. It's a bit like driving a car – you think that you'll never be able to do it and, when you master the art, you wonder how you ever managed to live without it!

The exercises in this book will take you slowly and smoothly through the functions of each program, ultimately introducing you to the more complex operations, and equipping you with the knowledge and skills necessary to use application programs efficiently in a business context.

You should work through this book, undertaking the exercises in sequence and checking your printouts thoroughly.

Before starting each lesson, arm yourself with a notebook, pen or pencil, and appropriate manuals or reference sheets. As you learn a new command, you should write the sequence in your notebook in order to have a permanent record for future reference. This will also help you in completing any theory exercise which you may be given.

It is good practice to write clearly on the printout which exercise you are submitting for checking, together with your name, class, date of submission and a brief summary of the commands which you have used in this exercise. This not only assists your tutor but also means that you have an accurate record of what you have achieved to date and an indication of what you still need to learn.

Everyone has to start somewhere, so read the explanations and instructions carefully, stay calm and confident, and you will be surprised at how efficient you can become.

Assessments

Assessments will be given by your tutor. These should be undertaken carefully and each instruction checked off as it is undertaken. All assessments should be undertaken and printouts submitted for checking as specified above. An Assessment Assignment is included at the end of the book which you may be able to use for practice material. Your tutor will advise you whether you should do this.

Word processing exercises

What is a Word Processing program?

Basically, a Word Processing program is a computer program which allows you to enter and edit text. Anything which would be done on a typewriter can normally be entered into a word processing program. Even good typists make mistakes, but by using a word processing program you can correct your work quickly and easily and have perfect documents every time. You can even check your spelling, so there is no risk of documents being sent out with errors.

There is really no need to worry about using a word processing program and most people who have been reluctant to use one in the first instance would never be without one now. A word processing program will usually make a copy of your file, shown in the file directory as a .BAK file so, if you do get into difficulties, you always have your 'back-up' file to save the day.

What can a word processing system do?

- It allows you to edit (make changes) to your document at any time
- It allows you to spell check your document
- It allows you to move text from one location to another
- It allows you to change margins, embolden, underline, etc
- It allows you to merge two documents
- It allows you to copy text from one file into another
- It allows you to alter fonts (ie character size/appearance)
- It allows you automatically to centre text (top and bottom as well as between margins)

And much more! You are limited only by the program which you are using!

Examples of popular word processing programs are:

WordStar · Multimate · DisplayWrite · WordPerfect · Word

Summary

Word processing is an application program which allows you to enter text and thereafter to edit it as required, displaying it effectively.

Summary of new commands used in each exercise

The following is a summary of the commands you will need to know prior to commencing each exercise. Please check with your tutor or consult your manual for advice where necessary.

Exercise 1   Basic text entering/editing skills · Spell checking · Saving and printing

Exercise 1.1   File retrieving · Editing and reforming commands

Exercise 2   Consolidation of previously learned commands

Exercise 2.1   Changing margins

Exercise 2.2   Line spacing

Word Processing Exercise 1

Enter the following text in single line spacing, correcting your typing errors as you go along. On completion, run a spell check on your document before saving as EX1 and printing a copy.

If you are new to word processing, there are a few simple rules which you should follow.

Firstly, you should always name your documents according to the information which they contain. There is nothing worse than trying to find a file months later when you cannot remember what you called it.

Secondly, you should always proofread everything prior to saving and printing. Of invaluable assistance is the spell check facility. Using this feature the program loads the UK English dictionary and proceeds to check your spelling throughout the entire document. Unfortunately, it also picks out proper names and technical information which is not contained in its memory.

Lastly, never erase anything without firstly considering carefully whether or not you really want to do this. Can you imagine a whole day's work wasted because of one mistake!

Word Processing Exercise 1.1

Recall Exercise 1 and make the following amendments to it. On completion spell check, save as EX1.1 and print a copy of your work.

If you are new to word processing, there are a few simple

rules which you should follow.

Firstly, you should always name your documents according to

the information which they contain. There is nothing worse

than trying to find *locate* a file months later when you cannot

remember what you called it.

Secondly, you should always proofread everything prior to

saving and printing. Of invaluable assistance is the spell

check facility. Using this feature/ the program loads the UK

English dictionary and proceeds to check your spelling

throughout the entire document. Unfortunately, it also picks

out proper names and technical information which ~~is~~ *it does* not

contain~~ed in its memory~~.

Lastly, never erase anything without ~~firstly~~ considering

carefully whether or not you really want to do this. ~~Can you~~

Imagine a whole day's work wasted because of one mistake!

Word Processing Exercise 2

Enter the following text in double line spacing, correcting your typing errors as you go along. On completion, run a spell check on your document before saving as EX2 and printing a copy.

Once you have been using a word processing program for a reasonable period of time, you will become more confident and competent in its use.

Never be afraid to try new features but bear in mind that it is always a good idea to take a copy of the file prior to trying out anything new for the first time.

Good file management is important in computing and files which are no longer required should be erased from the disk in order to make room for new ones. It is often a good idea to remove back-up files from the disk if they are no longer required since this can give you considerably more disk space available. These files usually have a .BAK extension. However, these files can be useful if you accidently erase a file which you really meant to keep.

Word Processing Exercise 2.1

Recall Exercise 2, change the left-hand margin to 1.5" (38 mm) and make the following amendments to the text (changing to single line spacing). On completion, spell check, save as EX2.1 and print a copy of your work.

Once you have been using a word processing program for a

reasonable period of time, you will become more confident and

competent in its use.

Never be afraid to try new features but bear in mind that it

is always a good idea to take a copy of the file prior to

trying out anything new for the first time.

Good file management is important in computing and files which

are no longer required should be erased from the disk in order

to make room for new ones. It is often a good idea to remove

back-up files from the disk if they are no longer required

since this can give you considerably more disk space

available. These files usually have a .BAK extension. on disk

However, these files can be useful if you accidently erase a

file which you really meant to keep.

Word Processing Exercise 2.2

Recall Exercise 2.1 and change the text into double line spacing and the margins to the original margins of 1" (25 mm). On completion, save as EX2.2 and print a copy of your work.

Word Processing Exercise 3

Enter the following letter with justification off, correcting your typing errors as you go along. On completion, run a spell check on your document prior to saving as EX3 and print a copy.

Today's Date

Mrs J Browne
Glebe House
GREATSFORD
Lincs
PE5 1RR

Dear Mrs Browne

Thank you for supplying us with written confirmation of your reservation.

We have pleasure in confirming that a double room with en suite bathroom will be reserved in your name for the nights of 18 and 19 December. The room will be at your disposal from 12 noon and we ask that you vacate the room by 11.30 am on the day of departure.

The cost of the room is £49.50, which includes full English or continental breakfast and VAT.

Dinner is served from 7.30 to 8.30 pm and reservations should be made by 3 pm on the day it is required.

We look forward to seeing you in December.

Yours sincerely

Miss F Sharman
Reservations Manager

Word Processing Exercise 3.1

Recall Exercise 3 and make the following amendments. Set justification on. On completion, check your spelling, save as EX3.1 and print copy of your document.

Today's Date

Mrs J Browne
Glebe House
GREATSFORD
Lincs
PE5 1RR

Dear Mrs Browne

Thank you for ~~supplying us~~ *your letter* with written confirmation of your reservation.

We have pleasure in confirming that a double room with en suite bathroom will be reserved in your name for the nights of 18 and 19 December. The room will be at your disposal from 12 noon and we ask that you vacate the room by 11.30 am on the day of departure.

The cost of the room is £49.50 *per night*, which includes full English or continental breakfast and VAT.

Dinner is served from 7.30 to 8.30 pm and reservations should be made by 3 pm on the day it is required.

We look forward to seeing you in December.

Yours sincerely

Miss F Sharman
Reservations Manager

8

Word Processing Exercise 4

Enter the following text, with justification on, correcting your typing errors as you go along. On completion, run a spell check on your document prior to saving as EX4 and printing.

What does the year ahead hold? Or for that matter the decade which will take us up to a new century?

None of us knows exactly what will happen but we may hazard a few guesses, speculate as to the likelihood of certain things which will change irrevocably how we live our lives.

It doesn't require much imagination to say that women, more and more, will occupy positions of influence and power. But some job opportunities remain a virtual all-male enclave. There are women lawyers, even women Sheriffs, but how many women on the bench of Britain's highest courts? Will that change before the next century?

And what about the house-husband of the nineties? Seeing to the more domestic tasks - purchasing the groceries, cleaning the house, doing the washing and the ironing and so on. Will we see more of that during the next few years?

Word Processing Exercise 4.1

Recall Exercise 4 and, using a left-hand margin of 1.5" (38 mm), make the following amendments. On completion, check your spelling, save as EX4.1 and print a copy of your document.

---

① What does the year ahead hold? Or for that matter the decade which will take us up to a new century?

② None of us knows exactly what will happen but we may hazard a few guesses, speculate as to the likelihood of certain things which will change irrevocably how we live our lives.

④ It doesn't require much imagination to say that women, more and more, will occupy positions of influence and power. But some job opportunities remain a virtual all-male enclave. There are women lawyers, even women Sheriffs, but how many women on the bench of Britain's highest courts? Will that change before the next century?

③ ♂ u.c. And what about the house-husband of the nineties? Seeing to the more domestic tasks - purchasing the groceries, cleaning the house, doing the washing and the ironing and so on. Will we see more of that during the next few years?

run on

It is comparatively recently that many men have been encouraged to accompany their wives when shopping or even take on the task single-handed.

With justification off, key in the following letter. On completion, save as EX5.

Suitable Reference

Today's Date

Mr M Richardson
17 Ashton Grove
YORK
YK5 5SD

Dear Mr Richardson

HOLIDAY TO TENERIFE

Thank you for your enquiry about the above holiday.

The departure date is 24 December at 11 am and the return date
is 12 January.

The price of £369 includes full board, bed and breakfast, in a
sea-facing room with en suite bathroom.

I trust that this meets with your immediate requirements.
Should you require any further assistance, however, please do
not hesitate to contact me.

Yours sincerely

Margaret Bain
Sales Manager

Word Processing Exercise 5.1

Recall Exercise 5 and make the following alterations to the text. On completion, save as EX5.1 and print a copy of your document.

Suitable Reference

Today's Date

Mr M Richardson
17 Ashton Grove
YORK
YK5 5SD

Dear Mr Richardson

HOLIDAY TO ~~TENERIFE~~ PORTUGAL

Thank you for your enquiry / yesterday about the above holiday.

The departure date is 24 December at ~~11 am~~ 1100 hours and the return date is 12 January.

The price of £369 includes full board, bed and breakfast, in a sea-facing room with en suite bathroom.

I trust that this meets with your immediate requirements. Should you require any further assistance, however, please do not hesitate to contact me.

Yours sincerely

Margaret Bain
Sales Manager

Word Processing Exercise 6

Using margins of 1.5" (38 mm), key in the following text in single line spacing. On completion, save as EX6 and print a copy of your document.

Accessories are an integral part of fashion, and you can easily update last year's clothes or that sale bargain with a change of buttons, the addition of a scarf or wrap, and the judicious use of a piece of jewellery.

The accessory that makes your outfit come alive can often give an individual aura to your dress sense.

The fact is that fashion accessories from belts to boots and bags are an inexpensive way of extending the life of your existing wardrobe.

Word Processing Exercise 6.1

Recall Exercise 6 and make the following alterations to text. Change to double line spacing. On completion, save as EX6.1 and print a copy of your document.

Accessories are an integral part of fashion, ~~and~~ which you can easily update. Last year's clothes or that sale u.c. bargain with a change of buttons, the addition of a scarf or wrap, and the judicious use of a piece of jewellery, can look like a completely new outfit. be made to

The accessory that makes your outfit come alive can often give an individual aura to your dress sense.

The fact is that fashion accessories from belts to boots and bags are an inexpensive way of extending the life of your existing wardrobe.

13

Word Processing Exercise 7

Key in the following text in single line spacing and justification on. On completion, save as EX7 and print a copy of your document.

Sunseekers are heading further afield as more long-haul trips are being booked.

The United States and Canada are the most popular resorts, with fly-drive to Florida being a favourite. Expensive cruises in the Caribbean and Mediterranean are being demanded more and more. Also in demand are trips to the far eastern cities of Bangkok, Hong Kong and Tokyo.

Spain is still popular but not as much visited as before. The popular European resorts are in Cyprus and Yugoslavia and holidays in the Canary Islands of Lanzarotte and Tenerife are now firm favourites with the British.

Recall Exercise 7 and make the following alterations to text. Change to double line spacing and margins of 1.5" (38 mm). Remove justification of right margin. On completion, save as EX7.1 and print a copy of your document.

Sunseekers are heading further afield as more long-haul trips are being booked.

The United States and Canada are the most popular resorts, with fly-drive to Florida being a favourite. Expensive cruises in the Caribbean and Mediterranean are being demanded more and more. Also in demand are trips to the far eastern cities of Bangkok, Hong Kong and Tokyo.

Spain is still popular but not as much visited as before. The popular European resorts are in Cyprus and Yugoslavia and holidays in the Canary Islands of Lanzarotte and Tenerife are now firm favourites with the British. However, Spain & Greece still offer excellent value for money and will continue to do so for many years to come.

Word Processing Exercise 8

Key in the following table, using a mixture of flush left and decimal tab settings. On completion, save as EX8 and print a copy of your table.

SALES FIGURES - JANUARY-JUNE

MONTH	CENTRAL	STRATHCLYDE	HIGHLAND	FIFE	BORDERS
Jan	1230	1500	1520	1234	1120
Feb	1330	1231	1657	1234	1100
March	1230	1511	1200	1510	1600
April	1600	1100	1530	1110	1211
May	1177	1120	1000	1000	1341
June	1321	1345	900	1200	1211

Word Processing Exercise 8.1

Key in the following table, using a mixture of flush left and decimal tabs. Upon completion, save as EX8.1 and print a copy of your file.

SEAT SALE FARES (for travel until 13 March, travel completed by 20 March)

TO	FROM LONDON	GLASGOW	MANCHESTER
St Johns	419.95	-	-
Halifax	500.00	545.45	-
Gander	500.00	545.45	-
Montreal	319.45	399.50	-
Ottawa	319.00	399.50	-
Toronto	319.00	399.50	-
Winnipeg	379.00	-	-
Calgary	429.00	429.00	429.00
Edmonton	429.00	-	429.00
Vancouver	449.50	449.50	449.50

Weekend Supplement: £20.00 each way applies as follows:

UK to Canada - Saturday/Sunday
Canada to UK - Friday/Saturday

PLEASE NOTE: Transatlantic fares are subject to constant review and change by the airlines. If you wish to guarantee your fares, this can be done by making full payment at the time of booking. Subject to no alterations being made to your reservation - your costing is then assured.

Word Processing Exercise 8.2

Key in the following table, using a mixture of flush left and decimal tab settings. Save as EX8.2 and print a copy of your file.

SENIOR CITIZEN FARES

	26 Dec-13 May 15 Oct-14 Dec		14 May-08 Jul 17 Sept-14 Oct		09 Jul-16 Sept 15 Dec-25 Dec	
TO	LONDON	GLASGOW	LONDON	GLASGOW	LONDON	GLASGOW
St Johns	369.00	–	410.57	–	461.00	–
Halifax	369.00	369.00	410.00	410.00	461.00	461.00
Gander	369.00	**349.00**	410.00	410.00	461.00	–
Montreal	369.00	–	410.00	–	461.00	–
Vancouver	503.50	**503.50**	544.00	**544.00**	585.50	**585.50**
Edmonton	482.00	–	523.00	–	564.00	–

Special Offer:

Glasgow/London (Return)	99.00	99.00	109.00	109.00	125.00	125.00

(Excluding Monday/Friday flights when full fare will be applied)

Word Processing Exercise 8.3

Retrieve the table from Exercise 8.2, and make the following alterations.

SENIOR CITIZEN FARES

TO	26 Dec-13 May 15 Oct-14 Dec		14 May-08 Jul 17 Sept-14 Oct		09 Jul-16 Sept 15 Dec-25 Dec	
	LONDON	GLASGOW	LONDON	GLASGOW	LONDON	GLASGOW
St Johns	369.00	–	410.57	–	461.00	–
Halifax	369.00	369.00	410.00	410.00	461.00	461.00
Gander	369.00	**349.00**	410.00	410.00	461.00	–
Montreal	319.45 ~~369.00~~	–	410.00	–	461.00	–
Vancouver	449.50 ~~503.50~~	449.50 ~~503.50~~	544.00	**544.00**	585.50	**585.50**
Edmonton	429.00 ~~482.00~~	–	523.00	–	564.00	–

trs (transpose Vancouver and Edmonton)

Intake 'weekend supplement' details from Ex8.1 here.

Special Offer:

Glasgow/London (Return)	99.00	99.00	109.00	109.00	125.00	125.00

(Excluding Monday/Friday flights when full fare will be applied)

Intake 'please note' details from Ex 8.1 here.

Word Processing Exercise 9

Key in the following advertisement, changing fonts in order to display it effectively. On completion, save as EX9 and print one copy.

INTERNAL VACANCY

A D V E R T I S E M E N T

PC OPERATOR(S)

We **URGENTLY** require to recruit PC operator(s) capable of using the following PC software programs:

> DisplayWrite
> DBase III+
> Lotus 1-2-3
> Ventura

Operators will be expected to use an IBM PS2 system PC - although training will be given where required.

The successful candidate will be required to work a total of 15 hours per week (Monday to Friday).

Please reply by Friday (insert next Friday's date) at the latest.

Further information available from: **Jason Saunders**
                                         Personnel Dept

Please quote ref: WP303 on any correspondence.

Word Processing Exercise 9.1

Retrieve the display from Exercise 9 and, using the search and replace facility, change **PC** to **Personal Computer** throughout.
  Copy this text a second time on the same page, save and print a copy. Take a photocopy and guillotine this photocopy to give you:

One master (two copies on one page)
Two (A5 size) advertisements.

Word Processing Exercise 10

Key in these Minutes using the following facilities:

1 Font changes for headings
2 Header incorporating: Minute No 231
3 Footer incorporating: Prepared by Mrs E A Rae
4 Automatic paragraph/page numbering
5 Temporary indent for paragraph wrap
6 Required page breaks

W E S T W O O D   P R I M A R Y   S C H O O L

PARENT/TEACHER ASSOCIATION

MINUTES OF MEETING held in the Senior School Staff Room on
Wednesday, 1 March 19-- at 1930 hours.

PRESENT: Mr Wilkinson   (Chairperson)
                      Mr Morrison   (Vice Chairperson)
                      Mrs Duncan   (Treasurer)
                      Mrs Rae   (Secretary)

          <u>Parent Members</u>   <u>Teacher Members</u>

          Mrs Saunders   Miss Crabtree
          Dr MacKay   Mrs Smith
          Mrs Patterson   Mrs Thomson
                                      Mr Jones (Headmaster)

1 APOLOGIES   There were no apologies.

2 PREVIOUS MINUTES   The minutes of the previous meeting,
                      held on 1 January 19-- were read and
                      accepted by Committee.

3 MATTERS ARISING   3.1   SCHOOL BOARDS

                      Mr Wilkinson reported that
                      notification with regard to
                      the School Board meeting to
                      be held at Grange High
                      School was received rather
                      late. However, the PTA
                      Newsletter which went out
                      on Monday gave the relevant
                      details to parents.

Mrs Rae reported that notification with regard to a meeting to be held in Rivers Primary School on 14 February was also received too late and that she had written to the Secretary of the PTF requesting that all future correspondence be sent directly to the school and pointing out that the late arrival as the reason for no PTA members being present from the school. A copy of the Minutes of the Meeting was also requested for perusal by the Committee.

Mr Wilkinson also reported that he had received notification that about 80 parents would attend the meeting at the local high school on Tuesday, 7 March. It was agreed that the Video would be shown at the next Committee meeting and that this would take priority on the Agenda.

3.2 PLAYING FIELDS

Mr Wilkinson read letters which he had received from Mr Roberts of the LEC and Mr Crawford, MP (together with copies of correspondence received from the Education Department) with regard to the proposed playing fields.

The matter of making application to the European Social Fund was also discussed and it was decided that the Committee would await further correspondence from the LEC and Donald Crawford before making any approach to the ESF.

4 SOCIAL EVENT

Mr Wilkinson reported that approximately 100 attendees were expected and that arrangements for the supply of wine and glasses had been made and Mrs Duncan and Mrs Saunders had the food supplies under control.

Mr Jones will purchase all the necessary supplies from the Cash & Carry.

Mr Morrison gave a demonstration of how the "Race Night" activities would be operated and Mrs Smith volunteered to sell tickets (20p each).

It was agreed that the proceeds from one of the races would be donated to "Comic Relief".

5 SCHOOL BUS

5.1 Mr Wilkinson said that 25 parents had indicated an interest in running a bus from the west side to/from the school and the headmaster agreed to obtain names of children in this area from the class lists in order that further correspondence may be directed accordingly.

5.2 Mr Wilkinson also reported that he had been approached with regard to a similar service being available to/from the top end of town and it was agreed that a tear-off slip would be included on the next Newsletter requesting an indication of interest.

6 PLAY AREA

The matter of dogs fouling the footpath and play area was brought to the attention of the Committee. It was agreed that the Secretary would write, in the first instance, to the Director of the Environment indicating the Committee's concern and requesting appropriate action.

7 CAR PARKING

It was brought to the attention of the Committee that there was, once again, a problem with regard to cars parking too near to the school crossing areas, coupled with the additional problem of parents or guardians actually driving into the playground in order to collect/leave children. Although the drop off/pick up point is designated as the area beside the football area, this is in a very bad state and parents are reluctant to allow their children to cross over it.

It was decided that Mrs Rae would
write to Dr Smith, at the Education
Department, pointing out the
Committee's concern and requesting
that this area be maintained to a
reasonable standard.

8   PLAY AREA   It was reported that the "Red Ash"
                                 play area of the playground was
                                 particularly bad and required
                                 attention. The headmaster agreed to
                                 write requesting an inspection of the
                                 playground and for subsequent remedial
                                 treatment to be carried out. He also
                                 undertook to send out a reminder to
                                 the children that they should not play
                                 in this area until further notice.

9   GYM ACTIVITIES   The subject of activities undertaken
                                 in the gym period (ie running) being
                                 too strenuous for the children was
                                 raised. It was pointed out that this
                                 was not the policy of the gym teacher
                                 but rather of education in general.
                                 It is thought that children today are
                                 not fit enough due to general lack of
                                 exercise and the programme is designed
                                 to commence with a gradual build-up to
                                 2 minutes running.

10   SPRING FAYRE   The date of Saturday, 27 May was set
                                 for the Spring Fayre and this will be
                                 notified to parents in the next
                                 Newsletter and discussed further at
                                 the next meeting.

11   NEXT MEETING   The next meeting of the Parent/Teacher
                                 Association will be held on Wednesday,
                                 26 April 19-- at 1930 hours in the
                                 Senior School Staff Room.

                                 Chairperson ....

                                 Date ....

Word Processing Exercise 10.1

In this exercise the master file must not be edited. If your program does not have the facility to save
your amendments with a different file name, you should make a copy of your file and then edit the
copy.

   Retrieve the Minutes prepared in Exercise 10 and edit as follows:

1 Using the Search and Replace facility:
   Change PLAY AREA (item 6) to FOOTBALL/PLAY AREA
2 Amend the footer to read: Prepared by Mrs Elizabeth A Rae, Secretary
3 Set the page length to 50 and alter the page breaks as necessary
4 Print out a copy of this file without page numbers
5 Print out a second copy of this file, terminating after page 1.

Input the following standard letter. This letter can be merged with the data file from Database Exercise 1; alternatively the relevant data can be input into an appropriate data file for merge purposes. Variable information is shown in braces. You should also print labels/envelopes as required.

Suitable Reference

Today's Date

{Company Name}
{Address}
{Town}
{Postcode}

Dear Sirs

Change of Address

Please note that as from Monday (**insert next Monday's date here**) we will be located at our new premises - 22 Union Road, EDINBURGH, EH1 2HH.

The telephone number will remain the same, as will the fax and telex numbers.

We look forward to dealing with your orders at our new premises.

Yours faithfully

A Thomas
Customer Accounts Manager

Word Processing Exercise 11.1

Input the following standard letter. This letter should be stored in keystroke program form (macro).
On completion, save and print a copy of your macro file.

```
Dear

Further to your telephone call to this office, I now have
pleasure in confirming your organisation's training requirements
to be as follows:

Course:
Program:
Level:
Duration:
Delegates:
Date:

Our invoice is enclosed for your attention. Please note that
course fees are payable prior to course commencement.

I trust that this meets with your immediate requirements. Should
you have any queries, however, please do not hesitate to contact
me.

Yours sincerely



Douglas Smith
PC Consultant

Enc
```

Please send the above letter to the following:

Letter 1	*Letter 2*
Mr David Donaldson	Ms Lillian Shaw
Regional Controller	Accountant
Northern Supplies PLC	North West Equipment
2 March Lane	Highgate Way
ABERDEEN	ABERDEEN
AB1 3NN	AB3 4JH

Course:	Word Processing	Course:	Spreadsheet
Program:	WordStar	Program:	SuperCalc
Level:	Introductory	Level:	Advanced
Duration:	2 days	Duration:	1 day
Delegates:	4	Delegates:	6
Date:	21 March 19—	Date:	27 March 19—

Word Processing Exercise 11.2

Key in the following invoice format in keystroke program (macro) format. Use a macro for automatic calculation where appropriate. Display effectively, changing fonts as required. Print out a blank copy and then merge with the previous data file (Exercise 11.1). The price per delegate should be entered as £125 for WP courses and £150 for spreadsheet courses.

I N V O I C E

TO: DATE:

                                              VAT NO: 123 678 2200

Training as follows:

Course   Delegates   Unit Price   Total Price

                                               VAT @ 17.5%   _____

                                               Total Due

                                                              ===========

Terms: <u>**Course fees payable prior to course commencement**</u>

Key in the following memorandum, displaying it appropriately and using font changes for headings.

M E M O R A N D U M

TO: J C Smith   FROM: Paul Young

SUBJECT: Expenses   DATE: (Today's Date)

I detail below expenses incurred by myself during my recent visit to Geneva.

It would be most beneficial if I could receive payment of these expenses by Friday of next week since I am due to fly off to Vancouver on business on the following Monday.

(Insert Spreadsheet Exercise 3 here)

Key in the following report, laying it out attractively. On completion, save and print a copy of your file.

R E P O R T

on

CLASS 3C EXAMINATION RESULTS

I have studied carefully the examination results of class 3c and would give my comments as follows:

Subject	Class Average	Comments
History		A very good average mark indeed
Geography		Slightly poorer than last year but nonetheless very good
Maths		The highest class average for 3rd year
English		Markedly poorer than last year but I accept your comments that this may be due to curriculum changes
French		Much better than expected from 3c

The average class mark of Paul.   was most satisfying. Well done

(Intake appropriate cells entries from Spreadsheet Exercise 4)

Key in the following text using the superscript/subscript facility or alternatively the ASCII codes which are relevant to your software program.

WordStar Commands for Text Enhancement + Superscript & Subscript

The commands which you use to carry out these functions in WordStar are referred to as printer control commands. The text will not be displayed exactly as it will print - it may change colour if you have a colour monitor but it will print out as you have instructed. If your printer does not have the facility to print in half line spaces you may find that an extra line is inserted in order to accommodate the command.

Emboldening Text   In order to embolden text you should use the

command Ctrl PB before and after the text

which you wish to embolden.

Underscoring Text   In order to underscore text you should use

the command Ctrl PS before and after the

text which you wish to underscore.

^{Superscripting} Text   In order to superscript text you should use

the command Ctrl PT before and after the

text which you wish to superscript.

$_{Subscripting}$ Text   In order to subscript text you should use

the command Ctrl PV before and after the

text which you wish to subscript.

Retrieve Exercise 14, searching for Ctrl and replacing it with Ctrl (ˆ). Amend the line spacing, and amend the subscript and superscript as indicated, and remove the final sentence from the first paragraph.

<u>**WordStar Commands for Text Enhancement**</u>
<u>**+ Superscript & Subscript**</u>

The commands which you use to carry out these functions in WordStar are referred to as printer control commands. The text will not be displayed exactly as it will print - it may change colour if you have a colour monitor but it will print out as you have instructed. If your printer does not have the facility to print in half line spaces you may find that an extra line is inserted in order to accommodate the command.

Emboldening Text

In order to embolden text you should use the command Ctrl PB before and after the text which you wish to embolden.

<u>Underscoring Text</u>

In order to underscore text you should use the command Ctrl PS before and after the text which you wish to underscore.

Superscripting ^{Text}

In order to superscript text you should use the command Ctrl PT before and after the text which you wish to superscript.

Subscripting $_{Text}$

In order to subscript text you should use the command Ctrl PV before and after the text which you wish to subscript.

Word Processing Exercise 15

In order that your information may be read by other programs, it is sometimes necessary to save your file to disk in what is commonly referred to ASCII format, rather than save it as a Word Processing format file (ASCII is short for American Standard Computer Information Code and allows the information on a disk to be understood and used by another make of computer.)

Retrieve the file saved as EX5 and transfer it to ASCII format. Then print out a copy of your file.

Please note that your file should be printed from DOS using the appropriate DOS print command.

Word Processing Exercise 16

You are required to make security copies (back-ups) of the following files – preferably on a different disk):

Exercise 3   Exercise 8   Exercise 10

On completion, print a copy of your file directory, using the print screen key or command if required.

Word processing solutions

Word Processing Exercise 1

If you are new to word processing, there are a few simple
rules which you should follow.

Firstly, you should always name your documents according to
the information which they contain. There is nothing worse
than trying to find a file months later when you cannot
remember what you called it.

Secondly, you should always proofread everything prior to
saving and printing. Of invaluable assistance is the spell
check facility. Using this feature the program loads the UK
English dictionary and proceeds to check your spelling
throughout the entire document. Unfortunately, it also picks
out proper names and technical information which is not
contained in its memory.

Lastly, never erase anything without firstly considering
carefully whether or not you really want to do this. Can you
imagine a whole day's work wasted because of one mistake!

Word Processing Exercise 1.1

If you are new to word processing, there are a few simple
rules which you should follow.

Firstly, you should always name your documents according to
the information which they contain. There is nothing worse
than trying to locate a file months later when you cannot
remember what you called it.

Secondly, you should always proofread everything prior to
saving and printing. Of invaluable assistance is the spell
check facility. Using this feature, the program loads the UK
English dictionary and proceeds to check your spelling
throughout the entire document. Unfortunately, it also picks
out proper names and technical information which it does not
contain.

Lastly, never erase anything without considering carefully
whether or not you really want to do this. Imagine a whole
day's work wasted because of one mistake!

Word Processing Exercise 2

Once you have been using a word processing program for a reasonable period of time, you will become more confident and competent in its use.

Never be afraid to try new features but bear in mind that it is always a good idea to take a copy of the file prior to trying out anything new for the first time.

Good file management is important in computing and files which are no longer required should be erased from the disk in order to make room for new ones. It is often a good idea to remove back-up files from the disk if they are no longer required since this can give you considerably more disk space available. These files usually have a .BAK extension. However, these files can be useful if you accidently erase a file which you really meant to keep.

Word Processing Exercise 2.1

Once you have been using a word processing program for a reasonable period of time, you will become more confident and competent in its use.

Never be afraid to try new features but bear in mind that it is always a good idea to take a copy of the file prior to trying out anything for the first time.

Good file management is important in computing and files which are no longer required should be erased from the disk in order to make room for new ones. It is often a good idea to remove back-up files from the disk if they are no longer required since this can give you considerably more space available on disk. These files usually have a .BAK extension. However, they can be useful if you accidently erase a file which you really meant to keep.

Word Processing Exercise 2.2

Once you have been using a word processing program for a
reasonable period of time, you will become more confident and
competent in its use.

Never be afraid to try new features but bear in mind that it
is always a good idea to take a copy of the file prior to
trying out anything for the first time.

Good file management is important in computing and files which
are no longer required should be erased from the disk in order
to make room for new ones. It is often a good idea to remove
back-up files from the disk if they are no longer required
since this can give you considerably more space available on
disk. These files usually have a .BAK extension. However,
they can be useful if you accidently erase a file which
you really meant to keep.

Word Processing Exercise 3

Today's Date

Mrs J Browne
Glebe House
GREATSFORD
Lincs
PE5 1RR

Dear Mrs Browne

Thank you for supplying us with written confirmation of your reservation.

We have pleasure in confirming that a double room with en suite bathroom will be reserved in your name for the nights of 18 and 19 December. The room will be at your disposal from 12 noon and we ask that you vacate the room by 11.30 am on the day of departure.

The cost of the room is £49.50, which includes full English or continental breakfast and VAT.

Dinner is served from 7.30 to 8.30 pm and reservations should be made by 3 pm on the day it is required.

We look forward to seeing you in December.

Yours sincerely

Miss F Sharman
Reservations Manager

Word Processing Exercise 3.1

Today's Date

Dear Mrs Browne

Thank you for your letter with written confirmation of your reservation.

We have pleasure in confirming that a double room with en suite bathroom will be reserved in your name for the nights of 18 and 19 December. The room will be at your disposal from 12 noon and we ask that you vacate the room by 11.30 am on the day of departure.

Dinner is served from 7.30 to 8.30 pm and reservations should be made by 3 pm on the day it is required.

The cost of the room is £49.50 per night, which includes full English or continental breakfast and VAT.

We look forward to seeing you in December.

Yours sincerely

Miss F Sharman
Reservations Manager

Mrs J Browne
Glebe House
GREATSFORD
Lincs
PE5 1RR

Word Processing Exercise 4

What does the year ahead hold? Or for that matter the decade which will take us up to a new century?

None of us knows exactly what will happen but we may hazard a few guesses, speculate as to the likelihood of certain things which will change irrevocably how we live our lives.

It doesn't require much imagination to say that women, more and more, will occupy positions of influence and power. But some job opportunities remain a virtual all-male enclave. There are women lawyers, even women Sheriffs, but how many women on the bench of Britain's highest courts? Will that change before the next century?

And what about the house-husband of the nineties? Seeing to the more domestic tasks - purchasing the groceries, cleaning the house, doing the washing and the ironing and so on. Will we see more of that during the next few years?

Word Processing Exercise 4.1

What does the year ahead hold? Or for that matter the decade which will take us up to a new century?

None of us knows exactly what will happen but we may hazard a few guesses, speculate as to the likelihood of certain things which will change irrevocably how we live our lives.

What about the house-husband of the nineties? Seeing to the more domestic tasks - purchasing the groceries, cleaning the house, doing the washing and the ironing and so on. Will we see more of that during the next few years? It is comparatively recently that many men have been encouraged to accompany their wives when shopping or even take on the task single-handed.

It doesn't require much imagination to say that women, more and more, will occupy positions of influence and power. But some job opportunities remain a virtual all-male enclave. There are women lawyers, even women Sheriffs, but how many women on the bench of Britain's highest courts? Will that change before the next century?

Word Processing Exercise 5

Suitable Reference

Today's Date

Mr M Richardson
17 Ashton Grove
YORK
YK5 5SD

Dear Mr Richardson

HOLIDAY TO TENERIFE

Thank you for your enquiry about the above holiday.

The departure date is 24 December at 11 am and the return date
is 12 January.

The price of £369 includes full board, bed and breakfast, in a
sea-facing room with en suite bathroom.

I trust that this meets with your immediate requirements.
Should you require any further assistance, however, please do
not hesitate to contact me.

Yours sincerely

Margaret Bain
Sales Manager

Word Processing Exercise 5.1

Suitable Reference

Today's Date

Dear Mr Richardson

HOLIDAY TO PORTUGAL

Thank you for your enquiry yesterday about the above holiday.

The price of £369 includes full board, bed and breakfast, in a sea-facing room with en suite bathroom.

The departure date is 24 December at 1100 hours and the return date is 12 January.

I trust that this meets with your immediate requirements. Should you require any further assistance, however, please do not hesitate to contact me.

Yours sincerely

Margaret Bain
Sales Manager

Mr M Richardson
17 Ashton Grove
YORK
YK5 5SD

Word Processing Exercise 6

Accessories are an integral part of fashion, and you can easily update last year's clothes or that sale bargain with a change of buttons, the addition of a scarf or wrap, and the judicious use of a piece of jewellery.

The accessory that makes your outfit come alive can often give an individual aura to your dress sense.

The fact is that fashion accessories from belts to boots and bags are an inexpensive way of extending the life of your existing wardrobe.

Word Processing Exercise 6.1

Accessories are an integral part of fashion, which you can easily update. Last year's clothes or that sale bargain with a change of buttons, the addition of a scarf or wrap, and the judicious use of a piece of jewellery, can be made to look like a completely new outfit.

The fact is that fashion accessories from belts to boots and bags are an inexpensive way of extending the life of your existing wardrobe.

The accessory that makes your outfit come alive can often give an individual aura to your dress sense.

Word Processing Exercise 7

Sunseekers are heading further afield as more long-haul trips are being booked.

The United States and Canada are the most popular resorts, with fly-drive to Florida being a favourite. Expensive cruises in the Caribbean and Mediterranean are being demanded more and more. Also in demand are trips to the far eastern cities of Bangkok, Hong Kong and Tokyo.

Spain is still popular but not as much visited as before. The popular European resorts are in Cyprus and Yugoslavia and holidays in the Canary Islands of Lanzarotte and Tenerife are now firm favourites with the British.

Word Processing Exercise 7.1

Sunseekers are heading further afield as more long-haul trips are being booked.

The United States and Canada are the most popular resorts, with fly-drive to Florida being a favourite. Expensive cruises in the Caribbean and Mediterranean are being demanded more and more. Also in demand are trips to the far eastern cities of Bangkok, Hong Kong and Tokyo. Spain is still popular but not as much visited as before.

The popular European resorts are in Cyprus and Yugoslavia and holidays in the Canary Islands of Lanzarotte and Tenerife are now firm favourites with the British. Spain is still popular but not as much visited as before. However, Spain and Greece still offer excellent value for money and will continue to do so for many years to come.

Word Processing Exercise 8

SALES FIGURES - JANUARY-JUNE

MONTH	CENTRAL	STRATHCLYDE	HIGHLAND	FIFE	BORDERS
Jan	1230	1500	1520	1234	1120
Feb	1330	1231	1657	1234	1100
March	1230	1511	1200	1510	1600
April	1600	1100	1530	1110	1211
May	1177	1120	1000	1000	1341
June	1321	1345	900	1200	1211

Word Processing Exercise 8.1

SEAT SALE FARES   (for travel until 13 March, travel completed by 20 March)

TO	FROM LONDON	GLASGOW	MANCHESTER
St Johns	419.95	-	-
Halifax	500.00	545.45	-
Gander	500.00	545.45	-
Montreal	319.45	399.50	-
Ottawa	319.00	399.50	-
Toronto	319.00	399.50	-
Winnipeg	379.00	-	-
Calgary	429.00	429.00	429.00
Edmonton	429.00	-	429.00
Vancouver	449.50	449.50	449.50

Weekend Supplement: £20.00 each way applies as follows:

UK to Canada - Saturday/Sunday
Canada to UK - Friday/Saturday

PLEASE NOTE: Transatlantic fares are subject to constant review
and change by the airlines. If you wish to
guarantee your fares, this can be done by making
full payment at the time of booking. Subject to no
alterations being made to your reservation - your
costing is then assured.

Word Processing Exercise 8.2

SENIOR CITIZEN FARES

TO	26 Dec-13 May 15 Oct-14 Dec		14 May-08 Jul 17 Sept-14 Oct		09 Jul-16 Sept 15 Dec-25 Dec	
	LONDON	GLASGOW	LONDON	GLASGOW	LONDON	GLASGOW
St Johns	369.00	-	410.57	-	461.00	-
Halifax	369.00	369.00	410.00	410.00	461.00	461.00
Gander	369.00	**349.00**	410.00	410.00	461.00	-
Montreal	369.00	-	410.00	-	461.00	-
Vancouver	503.50	**503.50**	544.00	**544.00**	585.50	**585.50**
Edmonton	482.00	-	523.00	-	564.00	-

Special Offer:

Glasgow/London (Return)	99.00	99.00	109.00	109.00	125.00	125.00

(Excluding Monday/Friday flights when full fare will be applied)

Word Processing Exercise 8.3

SENIOR CITIZEN FARES

TO	26 Dec-13 May 15 Oct-14 Dec		14 May-08 Jul 17 Sept-14 Oct		09 Jul-16 Sept 15 Dec-25 Dec	
	LONDON	GLASGOW	LONDON	GLASGOW	LONDON	GLASGOW
St Johns	369.00	–	410.57	–	461.00	–
Halifax	369.00	369.00	410.00	410.00	461.00	461.00
Gander	369.00	**349.00**	410.00	410.00	461.00	–
Montreal	319.45	–	410.00	–	461.00	–
Edmonton	429.00	–	523.00	–	564.00	–
Vancouver	449.50	**449.50**	544.00	**544.00**	585.50	**585.50**

Weekend Supplement: £20.00 each way applies as follows:

UK to Canada – Saturday/Sunday
Canada to UK – Friday/Saturday

Special Offer:

Glasgow/London (Return)	99.00	99.00	109.00	109.00	125.00	125.00

(**Excluding Monday/Friday flights when full fare will be applied**)

PLEASE NOTE: Transatlantic fares are subject to constant review and change by the airlines. If you wish to guarantee your fares, this can be done by making full payment at the time of booking. Subject to no alterations being made to your reservation – your costing is then assured.

INTERNAL VACANCY

ADVERTISEMENT

<u>PC OPERATOR(S)</u>

We **URGENTLY** require to recruit PC operator(s) capable of using the following PC software programs:

> *DisplayWrite*
> *DBase III+*
> *Lotus 1-2-3*
> *Ventura*

Operators will be expected to use an IBM PS2 system PC - although training will be given where required.

The successful candidate will be required to work a total of 15 hours per week (Monday to Friday).

Please reply by *Friday* (insert next Friday's date) at the latest.

Further information available from: **Jason Saunders**
                                          Personnel Dept

Please quote ref: WP303 on any correspondence.

INTERNAL VACANCY

ADVERTISEMENT

PERSONAL COMPUTER OPERATOR(S)

We **URGENTLY** require to recruit Personal Computer operator(s) capable of using the following Personal Computer software programs:

> *DisplayWrite*
> *DBase III+*
> *Lotus 1-2-3*
> *Ventura*

Operators will be expected to use an IBM PS2 system Personal Computer - although training will be given where required.

The successful candidate will be required to work a total of 15 hours per week (Monday to Friday).

Please reply by *Friday* (insert next Friday's date) at the latest.

Further information available from: **Jason Saunders**
                                        Personnel Dept

Please quote ref: WP303 on any correspondence.

INTERNAL VACANCY

ADVERTISEMENT

PERSONAL COMPUTER OPERATOR(S)

We **URGENTLY** require to recruit Personal Computer operator(s) capable of using the following Personal Computer software programs:

> *DisplayWrite*
> *DBase III+*
> *Lotus 1-2-3*
> *Ventura*

Operators will be expected to use an IBM PS2 system Personal Computer - although training will be given where required.

The successful candidate will be required to work a total of 15 hours per week (Monday to Friday).

Please reply by *Friday* (insert next Friday's date) at the latest.

Further information available from: **Jason Saunders**
                                        Personnel Dept

Please quote ref: WP303 on any correspondence.

Minute No 231

W E S T W O O D   P R I M A R Y   S C H O O L

PARENT/TEACHER ASSOCIATION

MINUTES OF MEETING held in the Senior School Staff Room on Wednesday, 1 March 19-- at 1930 hours.

PRESENT:

Mr Wilkinson	(Chairperson)
Mr Morrison	(Vice Chairperson)
Mrs Duncan	(Treasurer)
Mrs Rae	(Secretary)

Parent Members	Teacher Members
Mrs Saunders	Miss Crabtree
Dr MacKay	Mrs Smith
Mrs Patterson	Mrs Thomson
	Mr Jones (Headmaster)

1   *APOLOGIES*   There were no apologies.

2   *PREVIOUS MINUTES*   The minutes of the previous meeting, held on 1 January 19-- were read and accepted by Committee.

3   *MATTERS ARISING*   3.1   **SCHOOL BOARDS**

Mr Wilkinson reported that notification with regard to the School Board meeting to be held at Grange High School was received rather late. However, the PTA Newsletter which went out on Monday gave the relevant details to parents.

Prepared by Mrs E A Rae

Mrs Rae reported that notification with regard to a meeting to be held in Rivers Primary School on 14 February was also received too late and that she had written to the Secretary of the PTF requesting that all future correspondence be sent directly to the school and pointing out that the late arrival as the reason for no PTA members being present from the school. A copy of the Minutes of the Meeting was also requested for perusal by the Committee.

Mr Wilkinson also reported that he had received notification that about 80 parents would attend the meeting at the local high school on Tuesday, 7 March. It was agreed that the Video would be shown at the next Committee meeting and that this would take priority on the Agenda.

3.2 **PLAYING FIELDS**

Mr Wilkinson read letters which he had received from Mr Roberts of the LEC and Mr Crawford, MP (together with copies of correspondence received from the Education Department) with regard to the proposed playing fields.

The matter of making application to the European Social Fund was also discussed and it was decided that the Committee would await further correspondence from the LEC and Donald Crawford before making any approach to the ESF.

4 *SOCIAL EVENT*

Mr Wilkinson reported that approximately 100 attendees were expected and that arrangements for the supply of wine and glasses had been made and Mrs Duncan and Mrs Saunders had the food supplies under control.

Prepared by Mrs E A Rae

Mr Jones will purchase all the necessary supplies from the Cash & Carry.

Mr Morrison gave a demonstration of how the "Race Night" activities would be operated and Mrs Smith volunteered to sell tickets (20p each).

It was agreed that the proceeds from one of the races would be donated to "Comic Relief".

5 *SCHOOL BUS*

5.1 Mr Wilkinson said that 25 parents had indicated an interest in running a bus from the west side to/from the school and the headmaster agreed to obtain names of children in this area from the class lists in order that further correspondence may be directed accordingly.

5.2 Mr Wilkinson also reported that he had been approached with regard to a similar service being available to/from the top end of town and it was agreed that a tear-off slip would be included on the next Newsletter requesting an indication of interest.

6 *PLAY AREA*

The matter of dogs fouling the footpath and play area was brought to the attention of the Committee. It was agreed that the Secretary would write, in the first instance, to the Director of the Environment indicating the Committee's concern and requesting appropriate action.

7 *CAR PARKING*

It was brought to the attention of the Committee that there was, once again, a problem with regard to cars parking too near to the school crossing areas, coupled with the additional problem of parents or guardians actually driving into the playground in order to collect/leave children. Although the

Prepared by Mrs E A Rae

drop off/pick up point is designated as the area beside the football area, this is in a very bad state and parents are reluctant to allow their children to cross over it.

It was decided that Mrs Rae would write to Dr Smith, at the Education Department, pointing out the Committee's concern and requesting that this area be maintained to a reasonable standard.

8 *PLAY AREA*

It was reported that the "Red Ash" play area of the playground was particularly bad and required attention. The headmaster agreed to write requesting an inspection of the playground and for subsequent remedial treatment to be carried out. He also undertook to send out a reminder to the children that they should not play in this area until further notice.

9 *GYM ACTIVITIES*

The subject of activities undertaken in the gym period (ie running) being too strenuous for the children was raised. It was pointed out that this was not the policy of the gym teacher but rather of education in general. It is thought that children today are not fit enough due to general lack of exercise and the programme is designed to commence with a gradual build-up to 2 minutes running.

10 *SPRING FAYRE*

The date of Saturday, 27 May was set for the Spring Fayre and this will be notified to parents in the next Newsletter and discussed further at the next meeting.

11 *NEXT MEETING*

The next meeting of the Parent/Teacher Association will be held on Wednesday, 26 April 19-- at 1930 hours in the Senior School Staff Room.

Chairperson ....

Date ....

Prepared by Mrs E A Rae

Minute No 231

W E S T W O O D   P R I M A R Y   S C H O O L

PARENT/TEACHER ASSOCIATION

MINUTES OF MEETING held in the Senior School Staff Room on
Wednesday, 1 March 19-- at 1930 hours.

PRESENT: Mr Wilkinson   (Chairperson)
            Mr Morrison   (Vice Chairperson)
            Mrs Duncan   (Treasurer)
            Mrs Rae   (Secretary)

Parent Members	Teacher Members
Mrs Saunders	Miss Crabtree
Dr MacKay	Mrs Smith
Mrs Patterson	Mrs Thomson
	Mr Jones (Headmaster)

1 *APOLOGIES*   There were no apologies.

2 *PREVIOUS MINUTES*   The minutes of the previous meeting,
                held on 1 January 19-- were read and
                accepted by Committee.

Prepared by Mrs Elizabeth A Rae, Secretary

Minute No 231

3 *MATTERS ARISING* 3.1 **SCHOOL BOARDS**

Mr Wilkinson reported that
notification with regard to
the School Board meeting to
be held at Grange High
School was received rather
late. However, the PTA
Newsletter which went out
on Monday gave the relevant
details to parents.

Mrs Rae reported that
notification with regard to a
meeting to be held in Rivers
Primary School on 14 February
was also received too late and
that she had written to the
Secretary of the PTF requesting
that all future correspondence
be sent directly to the school
and pointing out that the late
arrival as the reason for no PTA
members being present from the
school. A copy of the Minutes
of the Meeting was also
requested for perusal by the
Committee.

Mr Wilkinson also reported that
he had received notification
that about 80 parents would
attend the meeting at the local
high school on Tuesday, 7 March.

Prepared by Mrs Elizabeth A Rae, Secretary

It was agreed that the Video would be shown at the next Committee meeting and that this would take priority on the Agenda.

3.2 **PLAYING FIELDS**

Mr Wilkinson read letters which he had received from Mr Roberts of the LEC and Mr Crawford, MP (together with copies of correspondence received from the Education Department) with regard to the proposed playing fields.

The matter of making application to the European Social Fund was also discussed and it was decided that the Committee would await further correspondence from the LEC and Donald Crawford before making any approach to the ESF.

4 *SOCIAL EVENT*

Mr Wilkinson reported that approximately 100 attendees were expected and that arrangements for the supply of wine and glasses had been made and Mrs Duncan and Mrs Saunders had the food supplies under control.

Prepared by Mrs Elizabeth A Rae, Secretary

Mr Jones will purchase all the necessary supplies from the Cash & Carry.

Mr Morrison gave a demonstration of how the "Race Night" activities would be operated and Mrs Smith volunteered to sell tickets (20p each).

It was agreed that the proceeds from one of the races would be donated to "Comic Relief".

5 *SCHOOL BUS*

5.1 Mr Wilkinson said that 25 parents had indicated an interest in running a bus from the west side to/from the school and the headmaster agreed to obtain names of children in this area from the class lists in order that further correspondence may be directed accordingly.

5.2 Mr Wilkinson also reported that he had been approached with regard to a similar service being available to/from the top end of town and it was agreed that a tear-off slip would be included on the next Newsletter requesting an indication of interest.

Prepared by Mrs Elizabeth A Rae, Secretary

Minute No 231

6 *FOOTBALL/PLAY AREA*   The matter of dogs fouling the footpath and play area was brought to the attention of the Committee. It was agreed that the Secretary would write, in the first instance, to the Director of the Environment indicating the Committee's concern and requesting appropriate action.

7 *CAR PARKING*   It was brought to the attention of the Committee that there was, once again, a problem with regard to cars parking too near to the school crossing areas, coupled with the additional problem of parents or guardians actually driving into the playground in order to collect/leave children. Although the drop off/pick up point is designated as the area beside the football area, this is in a very bad state and parents are reluctant to allow their children to cross over it.

It was decided that Mrs Rae would write to Dr Smith, at the Education Department, pointing out the Committee's concern and requesting that this area be maintained to a reasonable standard.

Prepared by Mrs Elizabeth A Rae, Secretary

Minute No 231

8 *PLAY AREA*

It was reported that the "Red Ash" play area of the playground was particularly bad and required attention. The headmaster agreed to write requesting an inspection of the playground and for subsequent remedial treatment to be carried out. He also undertook to send out a reminder to the children that they should not play in this area until further notice.

9 *GYM ACTIVITIES*

The subject of activities undertaken in the gym period (ie running) being too strenuous for the children was raised. It was pointed out that this was not the policy of the gym teacher but rather of education in general. It is thought that children today are not fit enough due to general lack of exercise and the programme is designed to commence with a gradual build-up to 2 minutes running.

10 *SPRING FAYRE*

The date of Saturday, 27 May was set for the Spring Fayre and this will be notified to parents in the next Newsletter and discussed further at the next meeting.

Prepared by Mrs Elizabeth A Rae, Secretary

Minute No 231

11 *NEXT MEETING*   The next meeting of the Parent/Teacher
                           Association will be held on Wednesday,
                           26 April 19-- at 1930 hours in the
                           Senior School Staff Room.

                           Chairperson ....

                           Date ....

Prepared by Mrs E A Rae

Minute No 231

W E S T W O O D   P R I M A R Y   S C H O O L

PARENT/TEACHER ASSOCIATION

MINUTES OF MEETING held in the Senior School Staff Room on Wednesday, 1 March 19-- at 1930 hours.

PRESENT:

Mr Wilkinson	(Chairperson)
Mr Morrison	(Vice Chairperson)
Mrs Duncan	(Treasurer)
Mrs Rae	(Secretary)

Parent Members	Teacher Members
Mrs Saunders	Miss Crabtree
Dr MacKay	Mrs Smith
Mrs Patterson	Mrs Thomson
	Mr Jones (Headmaster)

1 *APOLOGIES* There were no apologies.

2 *PREVIOUS MINUTES* The minutes of the previous meeting, held on 1 January 19-- were read and accepted by Committee.

Prepared by Mrs Elizabeth A Rae, Secretary

Word Processing Exercise 11 (standard letter)

AT/me

Today's Date

^F1^
^F2^
^F3^
^F4^

Dear Sirs

Change of Address

Please note that as from Monday, date, we will be located at our new premises - 22 Union Road, EDINBURGH, EH1 2HH.

The telephone number will remain the same, as will the fax and telex numbers.

We look forward to dealing with your orders at our new premises.

Yours faithfully

A Thomas
Customer Accounts Manager

```
Alderton & Simms Ltd^R
33 Ashton Rd^R
EDINBURGH^R
EH5 5QQ^R
^E
Thomson & Co^R
57 High St^R
ABERDEEN^R
AB1 1JT^R
^E
Andrews Bros^R
55 North Byers Rd^R
ABERDEEN^R
AB6 4PT^R
^E
Curtain Call^R
23 Coronation St^R
EDINBURGH^R
EH2 7HB^R
^E
Peebles Fashions Ltd^R
33 Mottles Green^R
LONDON^R
NW4^R
^E
```

Word Processing Exercise 11 (example of merged letter)

AT/me

Today's Date

Alderton & Simms Ltd
33 Ashton Rd
EDINBURGH
EH5 5QQ

Dear Sirs

Change of Address

Please note that as from Monday, date, we will be located at
our new premises - 22 Union Road, EDINBURGH, EH1 2HH.

The telephone number will remain the same, as will the fax and
telex numbers.

We look forward to dealing with your orders at our new
premises.

Yours faithfully

A Thomas
Customer Accounts Manager

Word Processing Exercise 11.1 (standard letter)

Dear

Further to your telephone call to this office, I now have pleasure in confirming your organisation's training requirements to be as follows:

Course:
Program:
Level:
Duration:
Delegates:
Date:

Our invoice is enclosed for your attention. Please note that course fees are payable prior to course commencement.

I trust that this meets with your immediate requirements. Should you have any queries, however, please do not hesitate to contact me.

Yours sincerely

Douglas Smith
PC Consultant

Enc

Word Processing Exercise 11.1 (letter 1)

DS/

Today's date

Mr David Donaldson
Regional Controller
Northern Supplies PLC
2 March Lane
ABERDEEN
AB1 3NN

Dear Mr Donaldson

Further to your telephone call to this office, I now have
pleasure in confirming your organisations's training
requirements to be as follows:

Course: Word Processing
Program: WordStar
Level: Introductory
Duration: 2 days
Delegates: 4
Date: 21 March 19--

Our invoice is enclosed for your attention. Please note that
course fees are payable prior to course commencement.

I trust that this meets with your immediate requirements.
Sould you have any queries, however, please do not hesitate to
contact me.

Yours sincerely

Douglas Smith
PC Consultant

Enc

Word Processing Exercise 11.1 (letter 2)

DS/

Today's date

Ms Lillian Shaw
Accountant
North West Equipment
Highgate Way
ABERDEEN
AB3 4JH

Dear Ms Shaw

Further to your telephone call to this office, I now have
pleasure in confirming your organisations's training
requirements to be as follows:

Course: Spreadsheet
Program: SuperCalc
Level: Advanced
Duration: 1 day
Delegates: 6
Date: 27 March 19--

Our invoice is enclosed for your attention. Please note that
course fees are payable prior to course commencement.

I trust that this meets with your immediate requirements.
Sould you have any queries, however, please do not hesitate to
contact me.

Yours sincerely

Douglas Smith
PC Consultant

Enc

Word Processing Exercise 11.2

                    I N V O I C E

TO: DATE:

                              VAT NO: 123 678 2200
_____

Training as follows:

Course   Delegates   Unit Price   Total Price

                                  VAT @ 17.5%   _____

                                  Total Due
                                              ============

Terms: <u>Course fees payable prior to course commencement</u>

I N V O I C E

TO: Mr David Donaldson
Regional Controller
Northern Supplies PLC
2 March Lane
ABERDEEN
AB1 3NN

DATE: Today's date

VAT NO: **123 678 2200**

Training as follows:

Course	Delegates	Unit Price	Total Price
WordStar Word Processing	4	£125.00	£500.00

£87.50

VAT @ 17.5% _____

Total Due   £587.50

===========

Terms: <u>Course fees payable prior to course commencement</u>

I N V O I C E

TO: Ms Lillian Shaw
      Accountant
      North West Equipment
      Highgate Way
      ABERDEEN
      AB3 4JH

DATE: Today's date

VAT NO: 123 678 2200

Training as follows:

Course	Delegates	Unit Price	Total Price
SuperCalc Spreadsheet	6	£150.00	£900.00

	VAT @ 17.5%	£157.50
	Total Due	£1,057.50

===========

Terms: <u>Course fees payable prior to course commencement</u>

MEMORANDUM

TO:	J C Smith	**FROM:**	Paul Young
SUBJECT:	Expenses	**DATE:**	(Today's date)

I detail below expenses incurred by myself during my recent visit to Geneva.

It would be most beneficial if I could receive payment of these expenses by Friday of next week since I am due to fly off to Vancouver on business on the following Monday.

EXPENSE ACCOUNT - January/March

Expense	Jan	Feb	Mar	Total
Petrol	56.00	70.00	59.00	185.00
Entertainment	115.00	102.00	30.00	247.00
Child Minding	120.00	150.00	105.00	375.00
Travel	70.00	25.00	15.00	110.00
Sundry	45.00	31.00	20.000	96.00
TOTAL	406.00	378.00	229.00	1,013.00

R E P O R T

on

CLASS 3C EXAMINATION RESULTS

I have studied carefully the examination results of class 3c
and would give my comments as follows:

Subject	Class Average	Comments
History	77%	A very good average mark indeed
Geography	75%	Slightly poorer than last year but nonetheless very good
Maths	77%	The highest class average for 3rd year
English	72%	Markedly poorer than last year but I accept your comments that this may be due to curriculum changes
French	71%	Much better than expected from 3c

The average class mark of 74% was most satisfying. Well done
Paul.

<u>WordStar Commands for Text Enhancement</u>
<u>+ Superscript & Subscript</u>

The commands which you use to carry out these functions in WordStar are referred to as printer control commands. The text will not be displayed exactly as it will print - it may change colour if you have a colour monitor but it will print out as you have instructed. If your printer does not have the facility to print in half line spaces you may find that an extra line is inserted in order to accommodate the command.

Emboldening Text

In order to embolden text you should use the command Ctrl PB before and after the text which you wish to embolden.

<u>Underscoring Text</u>

In order to underscore text you should use the command Ctrl PS before and after the text which you wish to underscore.

Superscripting Text

In order to superscript text you should use the command Ctrl PT before and after the text which you wish to superscript.

Subscripting Text

In order to subscript text you should use the command Ctrl PV before and after the text which you wish to subscript.

<u>**WordStar Commands for Text Enhancement**</u>
<u>**+ Superscript & Subscript**</u>

The commands which you use to carry out these functions in WordStar are referred to as printer control commands. The text will not be displayed exactly as it will print - it may change colour if you have a colour monitor but it will print out as you have instructed.

Emboldening Text   In order to embolden text you should use the command Ctrl (^) PB before and after the text which you wish to embolden.

<u>Underscoring Text</u>   In order to underscore text you should use the command Ctrl (^) PS before and after the text which you wish to underscore.

Superscripting ^{Text}   In order to superscript text you should use the command Ctrl (^) PT before and after the text which you wish to superscript.

Subscripting _{Text}   In order to subscript text you should use the command Ctrl (^) PV before and after the text which you wish to subscript.

Desk top publishing exercises

What is a Desk Top Publishing system?

A Desk Top Publishing system enables the user to produce documents to a professional standard. You may enter and edit text, use bold, italic and underline, and practically every other function available in a word processing package. Desk Top Publishing, however, lets you go a step further, by allowing you to change font styles and sizes, add lines, shaded boxes and circles, and even bring in graphics from other packages. Thus, Desk Top Publishing allows you to produce an impressive document quickly and easily. Even a novice can create effective and professional-looking publications.

What can a Desk Top Publishing system do?

- It allows you to add and edit text
- It allows you to change margins, embolden, underline, etc.
- It allows you to add lines of varying thickness
- It allows you to add boxes, rounded corner boxes and circles of varying shades and line thickness
- It allows you to enlarge and reduce text
- It allows you to add text and graphics from other packages
- It allows you to move items around the page easily
- It allows you to place items on a master page so that they will appear on every page of the document
- It allows you to number pages automatically

Examples of popular Desk Top Publishing programs are:

Aldus PageMaker   Ventura

Summary

Desk Top Publishing allows you to create impressive professional-looking documentation quickly and easily.

Summary of new commands used in each exercise

The following is a summary of the commands you will need to know prior to commencing each exercise. Please check with your tutor or consult your manual for advice where necessary.

Exercise 1   Setting page setups · Opening a new file · Basic text entering skills · Saving and printing

Exercise 1.1   File retrieving · Editing text · Using centre, embolden and italic

Exercise 2   Placing text from a word processing package · Changing fonts

Exercise 2.1   Enlarging and reducing text size

Desk Top Publishing Exercise 1

Open a new Desk Top Publishing file and set up an A4 portrait style one page document with 30 mm margins all round. Enter in the following text, correcting your typing errors as you go. On completion save your document as DTP1 and print a copy.

Desk Top Publishing can be a very powerful tool to the user. It enables even a novice to create effective, professional-looking documentation without too much effort.

A document which is pleasing to the eye will entice a reader more than just columns of text, and splitting text using simple tools like lines and boxes will undoubtedly make the reader keener to look at the information you are trying to convey.

It is well known that people read VDU monitors less accurately than printed pages. Moreover, the VDU is unable to show artwork as effectively as the printed page. Producing a draft copy of your document before you decide on the final layout is a wise idea. This enables you to check each page individually and also to check the entire documentation for any errors which you may not have noticed onscreen.

Remember, save your documentation often. If you make a change which you decide you don't like or do something drastically wrong, then you can easily go back to one of your previous versions without having to start again from scratch.

Desk Top Publishing Exercise 1.1

Retrieve file DTP1 and make the following amendments to it. On completion, save your document as DTP1–1 and print a copy.

Make this a heading, centre and bold

DTP Packages

They enable

NP// Desk Top Publishing can be a very powerful tool to the user. ~~It enables~~ even a novice to create effective, professional-looking documentation without too much /effort. /*time and*

A document which is pleasing to the eye will entice a reader more than just columns of text, and splitting text using simple tools like lines and boxes will ~~undoubtedly~~ make the reader keener to look at the information you are trying to convey.

Make this whole paragraph italic

It is well known that people read VDU monitors less accurately than printed pages. Moreover, the VDU is unable to show artwork as effectively as the printed page. Producing a draft copy of your document before you decide on the final layout is a wise idea. This enables you to check each page individually and also to check the entire documentation for any errors which you may not have noticed onscreen.

Don't forget to

~~Remember,~~ save your documentation often. If you make a change which you decide you /*silly* don't like or do something /~~drastically wrong~~, then you can easily go back to one of your previous versions without having to start again from scratch.

Desk Top Publishing Exercise 2

Place Word Processing EX1.1 from your word processing files on to a new DTP file. Make the following amendments. Change the font to Helvetica or a similar style font, save the file as DTP2 and print a copy.

If you ~~are new to~~ *have never used a* word processing/*package* there are a few simple rules which you should follow.

make this word bold

Firstly, you should always name your documents according to **stet** the information ~~which they~~ contain. There is nothing worse than trying to locate a file months later when you cannot remember what you called it.

make this word bold

Secondly, you should always proofread everything prior to saving and printing. Of invaluable assistance is the spell check facility. Using this feature, the program loads the UK English dictionary and proceeds to check your spelling throughout the entire document. Unfortunately, it also picks out proper names and technical information which the dictionary does not contain.

make this word bold

Lastly, never erase anything without considering carefully whether or not you really want to do this. Imagine a whole day's work wasted because of one mistake!

Desk Top Publishing Exercise 2.1

Reopen DTP2 file and make the following amendments, save the file as DTP2-1 and print a copy.

Change first paragraph to 18pt text

If you have never used a word processing package, there are a few simple rules which you should follow.

NP // *change the rest of the text to 10pt except the words in bold*

Firstly, you should always name your documents according to the information which they contain. There is nothing worse than trying to locate a file months later when you cannot remember what you called it.

NP // **Secondly**, you should always proofread everything prior to saving and printing. Of invaluable assistance is the spell check facility. Using this feature, the program loads the UK English dictionary and proceeds to check your spelling throughout the entire document. Unfortunately, it also picks out proper names and technical information which the dictionary does not contain.

NP // **Lastly**, never erase anything without considering carefully whether or not you really want to do this. Imagine a whole day's work wasted because of one mistake!

Desk Top Publishing Exercise 2.2

Enter the following text in 12 point Times Roman text or similar (except where other fonts are indicated). Make the changes as you go and thereafter save as DTP2-2 and print a copy.

Put in a heading of "Animal Passion Fashion" in Times Roman 20pt Bold and Italics and centre it

make this paragraph Helvetica 14pt text or similar

This year the clothes are being ~~designed~~ *created* to bring out the beast in you ...

Lower case

Now Various different animal effect patterns available in Lycra are appearing in High Street shops ~~daily~~ *more and more frequently.* The range includes snake, tiger and zebra and they will be all the rage as you prowl around. The designers are trying to put a little fun into fashion this year and due to the recession they are also trying to keep the prices down.

add in the text from WP EX6 here in bold Helvetica 10 pt text or similar

Florals and pastels are still very popular for most but the more daring amongst us will soon be dazzling everyone in these new fabrics. Lycra looks stunning ... if you have a model figure, but unfortunately, for most of us it stretches out of recognition with our bulges!

make these words bold

Don't despair, though. There are always ways of wearing clothes to suit your particular figure. Fashion these days is all about adapting outfits to suit yourself.

So don't be a fashion victim ... look at what's available and then choose an outfit that will fit your figure best.

Open a copy of DTP1-1 and make the following amendments. Once completed, save as DTP3 and print a copy.

Draw a short 4pt line vertically on either side of the heading

Desk Top Publishing

DTP Packages can be a very powerful tool to the user. They enable even a novice to create effective, professional-looking documentation without too much time and effort.

A document which is pleasing to the eye will entice a reader more than just columns of text, and splitting text using simple tools like lines and boxes will make the reader keener to look at the information you are trying to convey.

Draw a 2pt horizontal line here from margin to margin

It is well known that people read VDU monitors less accurately than printed pages. Moreover, the VDU is unable to show artwork as effectively as the printed page. Producing a draft copy of your document before you decide on the final layout is a wise idea. This enables you to check each page individually and also to check the entire documentation for any errors which you may not have noticed onscreen.

Draw a 2pt horizontal line here from margin to margin

Don't forget to save your documentation often. If you make a change which you decide you don't like or do something silly, then you can easily go back to one of your previous versions without having to start again from scratch.

Draw a very heavy dotted line horizontally from margin to margin here

Open a copy of DTP3 and make the following amendments. Once completed, save as DTP3-1 and print a copy.

Remove these lines and replace with an unshaded box with a double line around it and the edges going all the way out to the margins

Desk Top Publishing

Draw a 10pt shaded box around the main body of text and remove the lines around it
DTP Packages can be a very powerful tool to the user. They enable even a novice to create effective, professional-looking documentation without too much time and effort.

A document which is pleasing to the eye will entice a reader more than just columns of text, and splitting text using simple tools like lines and boxes will make the reader keener to look at the information you are trying to convey.

It is well known that people read VDU monitors less accurately than printed pages. Moreover, the VDU is unable to show artwork as effectively as the printed page. Producing a draft copy of your document before you decide on the final layout is a wise idea. This enables you to check each page individually and also to check the entire documentation for any errors which you may not have noticed onscreen.

Don't forget to save your documentation often. If you make a change which you decide you don't like or do something silly, then you can easily go back to one of your previous versions without having to start again from scratch.

Desk Top Publishing Exercise 3.2

Enter the following on a page with 20 mm all round margins, in a Times Roman 12 pt font (or similar), making the changes as you go. Save as DTP3-2 and print a copy.

Draw a rounded corner 10pt unshaded box with a double line around heading

HIGHER/VOCATIONAL EDUCATION COMMITTEE

Change heading to → → Certificate

20pt Helvetica text or similar

The teaching of this certificate should be approached from the standpoint of the supervisor - a student-centred learning approach. This may be achieved by allowing the student to gain hands-on experience of a desk top publishing program progressively, with the tutor demonstrating new material and good working practice.

Move the entire paragraph

The use of audio-visual aids, together with visits to printers or design studios, could be incorporated and group work, where students explore the uses and problems of incorporating a desk top publishing program, is recommended.

The collecting of samples produced by software houses, eg books/manuals, could usefully be employed to help build an appreciation of design principles. Opportunities should be provided regularly for group discussions, particularly for the more aesthetic components of desk top publishing, and discussions on artistic qualities should be encouraged.

Acceptable performance will be satisfactory achievement of all aspects of the study area and the exact requirements of each section are clearly detailed in the summary sheet which has been issued to all centres.

Type in this paragraph at the bottom of the text and centre it. Put "Please note" in bold and draw box with no shading and a 4pt line around it right out to the margins.

Please note:
The above notes are only rough guidelines and do not have to be carried out verbatim.

Desk Top Publishing Exercise 4

Open a copy of DTP1 file. Move the zero point into the top corner of the right-hand margin and add in the following lines, using ruler lines to ensure that they are of equal spacing and length. Right justify the text. Save your document as DTP4 before printing a copy.

Add two carriage returns between each paragraph

Centre two 2pt horizontal lines of 9 cms long at this point on the page. The second line should be exactly 0.5 cm below the first.

Desk Top Publishing can be a very powerful tool to the user. It enables even a novice to create effective, professional-looking documentation without too much effort.

Copy the 9 cm lines ensuring that they are exactly in line vertically with those above

A document which is pleasing to the eye will entice a reader more than just columns of text, and splitting text using simple tools like lines and boxes will undoubtedly make the reader keener to look at the information you are trying to convey.

Copy the 9 cm lines ensuring that they are exactly in line vertically with those above

It is well known that people read VDU monitors less accurately than printed pages. Moreover, the VDU is unable to show artwork as effectively as the printed page. Producing a draft copy of your document before you decide on the final layout is a wise idea. This enables you to check each page individually and also to check the entire documentation for any errors which you may not have noticed onscreen.

Copy the 9 cm lines ensuring that they are exactly in line vertically with those above

Remember, save your documentation often. If you make a change which you decide you don't like or do something drastically wrong, then you can easily go back to one of your previous versions without having to start again from scratch.

Copy the 9 cm lines ensuring that they are exactly in line vertically with those above. Change the line width to 4pt.

Desk Top Publishing Exercise 4.1

Reopen DTP4 file. Change the leading (the space between the lines) to 1.5 times the font size, reposition the lines, save your file as DTP4-1 and print a copy.

Desk Top Publishing can be a very powerful tool to the user. It enables even a novice to create effective, professional-looking documentation without too much effort.

A document which is pleasing to the eye will entice a reader more than just columns of text, and splitting text using simple tools like lines and boxes will make the reader keener to look at the information you are trying to convey.

It is well known that people read VDU monitors less accurately than printed pages. Moreover, the VDU is unable to show artwork as effectively as the printed page. Producing a draft copy of your document before you decide on the final layout is a wise idea. This enables you to check each page individually and also to check the entire documentation for any errors which you may not have noticed onscreen.

Remember, save your documentation often. If you make a change which you decide you don't like or do something drastically wrong, then you can easily go back to one of your previous versions without having to start again from scratch.

Desk Top Publishing Exercise 5

Insert the following text from WP EX8.2 in Times Roman 12 pt text or similar font and set the tabs as instructed. Move the zero points into the top corner of the right-hand margin setting before beginning. Save as DTP5 and print a copy.

Make heading 22 pt Helvetica reverse text. Put in 100% shaded rounded corner box only around text, not out to margins.

SENIOR CITIZEN FARES

Centre tabs at 4.5 cm, 10 cm and 15 cm.

	26 Dec-13 May 14 Oct-14 Dec	14 May-08 Jul 17 Sept-14 Oct	09 Jul-16 Sept 15 Dec-25 Dec

Centre tabs at 4cm, 6cm, 9cm, 11cm, 14cm and 16cm.

TO	London	Glasgow	London	Glasgow	London	Glasgow

Decimal tabs at 4cm, 6cm, 9cm, 11cm, 14cm and 16cm.

TO	London	Glasgow	London	Glasgow	London	Glasgow
St Johns	369.00	–	410.57	–	461.00	–
Halifax	369.00	369.00	410.00	410.00	461.00	461.00
Gander	369.00	349.00	410.00	410.00	461.00	–
Montreal	369.00	–	410.00	–	461.00	–
Vancouver	503.50	503.50	544.00	544.00	585.50	585.50
Edmonton	482.00	–	523.00	–	564.00	–

Remove the lines and draw a box around the table with a 4 pt line. Use a 2 pt vertical line to split the "To" column from the rest.

<u>Special Offer</u>

Glasgow/London (Return)	99.00	99.00	109.00	109.00	125.00	125.00

<u>(Excluding Monday/Friday flights when full fare will be applied)</u>

Put this section in a box of its own, using the same width line as the box above.

86

Place the items indicated on your master page. Then type the text in 12 pt Helvetica (or similar) in double leading, starting a new page where indicated. Save your document as DTP5-1 and print a copy.

COMPUTER PROGRAMS

Put this on the master page *Box has a 6 pt line and 10% shading. Text is Helvetica 24 pt*

Word Processing is a computer program which allows you to enter and edit text. Anything which would be done on a typewriter can normally be entered into a word processing program. Even good typists make mistakes, but by using a word processing program you can have perfect copies every time. You can even check your spelling so there is no need to worry about documents being sent out with errors.

There is really no need to worry about using a word processing program and most people who have been reluctant to use one in the first instance would never be without one now. A word processing program will usually make what is called a .BAK file so, if you do get into difficulties, you always have your 'back-up' file to save the day.

Put the rest of the text on the next page

A Desk Top Publishing system enables the user to produce documents to a professional standard. You may enter and edit text, use bold, italic and underline, and practically every other function available in a word processing package.

Desk Top Publishing, however, lets you go a step further, by allowing you to change font styles and sizes, add lines, shaded boxes and circles, and even bring in graphics from other packages. Thus, Desk Top Publishing allows you to produce an impressive document quickly and easily. Even a novice can create effective and professional-looking publications.

Desk Top Publishing Exercise 5.2

Reopen DTP5-1. Add automatic page numbering and indented paragraphs where indicated. Save your document as DTP5-2 and print a copy.

COMPUTER PROGRAMS

Indent 1cm from here

(a) Word Processing is a computer program which allows you to enter and edit text. Anything which would be done on a typewriter can normally be entered into a word processing program. Even good typists make mistakes, but by using a word processing program you can have perfect copies every time. You can even check your spelling so there is no need to worry about documents being sent out with errors.

Indent 1cm from here

(b) There is really no need to worry about using a word processing program and most people who have been reluctant to use one in the first instance would never be without one now. A word processing program will usually make what is called a .BAK file so, if you do get into difficulties, you always have your 'back-up' file to save the day.

Add page numbers here

COMPUTER PROGRAMS

Indent 1cm from here

c) A Desk Top Publishing system enables the user to produce documents to a professional standard. You may enter and edit text, use bold, italic and underline, and practically every other function available in a word processing package.

Indent 1cm from here

d) Desk Top Publishing, however, lets you go a step further, by allowing you to change font styles and sizes, add lines, shaded boxes and circles, and even bring in graphics from other packages. Thus, Desk Top Publishing allows you to produce an impressive document quickly and easily. Even a novice can create effective and professional-looking publications.

Reproduce the following using tabs and ruler lines to help you. Save your document as DTP6 and print a copy.

ROYAL PRESERVATION FUND

Regional Examination Results

	Number of students	Average % gained this year	Average % gained over last 10 years
Cleveland	200	51.5	65
Greater Manchester	71	83.0	85
Lothian	158	74.6	86
Gwynedd	499	60.0	63
Inner London	1,333	46.9	49
Strathclyde	981	39.0	49
Manchester	5	98.3	93

These results show that students in most areas have gained slightly lower results than in previous years.

On more careful examination of the table we can deduce that students sitting exams in areas where the Preservation Fund exams are less popular tend to have a higher pass rate.

Reproduce the following chart, using ruler lines, etc, to help you. Save your document as DTP7 and print a copy.

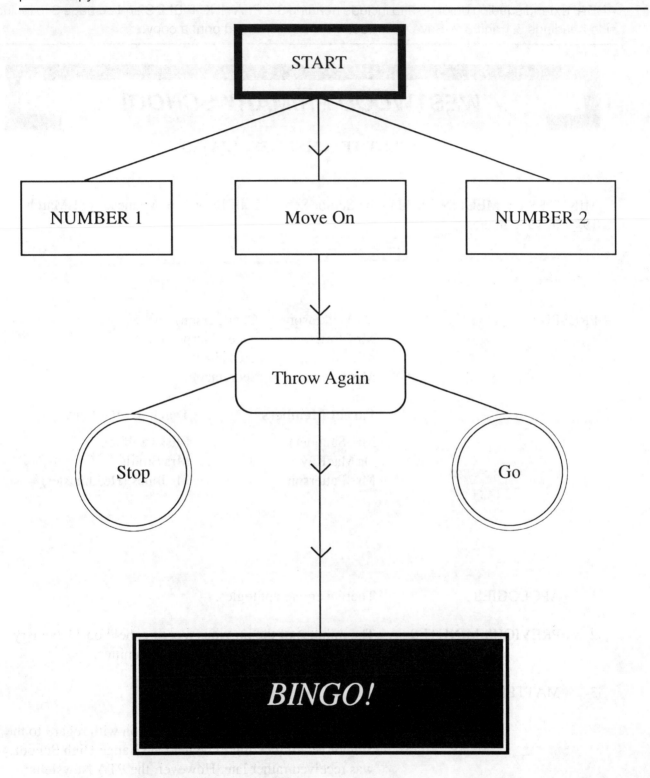

Place word processing exercise EX10 on to a new DTP file and reproduce it as follows. Remember to use the master page and indents where necessary. Alter item 6 PLAY AREA to read FOOTBALL AREA. Extend shading on page 2 to include heading 3.2 PLAYING FIELDS and on page 3 to include side headings 5.1 and 5.2. Save your document as DTP8 and print a copy.

WESTWOOD PRIMARY SCHOOL

PARENT/TEACHER ASSOCIATION

MINUTES OF MEETING held in the Senior School Staff Room on Wednesday, 1 March 19__ at 1930 hours.

PRESENT

Mr Wilkinson	(Chairperson)
Mr Morrison	(Vice Chairperson)
Mrs Duncan	(Treasurer)
Mrs Rae	(Secretary)

Parent Members	**Teacher Members**
Mrs Saunders	Miss Crabtree
Dr MacKay	Mrs Smith
Mrs Patterson	Mr Jones (Headmaster)

1   APOLOGIES   There were no apologies.

2   PREVIOUS MINUTES   The minutes of the previous meeting, held on 11 January 19__ were read and accepted by Committee.

3   MATTERS ARISING   **3.1   SCHOOL BOARDS**

Mr Wilkinson reported that notification with regard to the School Board meeting to be held at Grange High School was received rather late. However, the PTA Newsletter which went out on Monday gave the relevant details to parents.

1

WESTWOOD PRIMARY SCHOOL

PARENT/TEACHER ASSOCIATION

Mrs Rae reported that notification with regard to a meeting to be held in Rivers Primary School on 14 February was also received too late and that she had written to the Secretary of the PTF requesting that all future correspondence be sent directly to the school and pointing out that the late arrival was the reason for no PTA members being present from the school. A copy of the Minutes of the Meeting was also requested for perusal by the Committee.

Mr Wilkinson also reported that he had received notification that about 80 parents would attend the meeting at the local high school on Tuesday, 7 March.

It was agreed that the Video would be shown at the next Committee meeting and that this would take priority on the Agenda.

3.2 PLAYING FIELDS

Mr Wilkinson read letters which he had received from Mr Roberts of the LEC and Mr Crawford, MP (together with copies of correspondence received from the Education Department) with regard to the proposed playing fields.

The matter of making application to the European Social Fund was also discussed and it was decided that the Committee would await further correspondence from the LEC and Donald Crawford before making any approach to the ESF.

4   SOCIAL EVENT

Mr Wilkinson reported that approximately 100 attendees were expected and that arrangements for the supply of wine and glasses had been made, and Mrs Duncan and Mrs Saunders had the food supplies under control.

Mr Jones will purchase all the necessary supplies from the Cash & Carry.

Mr Morrison gave a demonstration of how the "Race Night" activities would be operated and Mrs Smith volunteered to sell tickets (20p each). It was agreed that the proceeds from one of the races would be donated to "Comic Relief".

WESTWOOD PRIMARY SCHOOL

PARENT/TEACHER ASSOCIATION

5   SCHOOL BUS

5.1   Mr Wilkinson said that 25 parents had indicated an interest in running a bus from the west side to/from the school and the headmaster agreed to obtain names of children in this area from the class lists in order that further correspondence may be directed accordingly.

5.2   Mr Wilkinson also reported that he had been approached with regard to a similar service being available to/from the top end of town and it was agreed that a tear-off slip would be included on the next Newsletter requesting an indication of interest.

6   FOOTBALL AREA

The matter of dogs fouling the footpath and play area was brought to the attention of the Committee. It was agreed that the Secretary would write, in the first instance, to the Director of the Environment indicating the Committee's concern and requesting appropriate action.

7   CAR PARKING

It was brought to the attention of the Committee that there was, once again, a problem with regard to cars parking too near to the school crossing areas, coupled with the additional problem of parents or guardians actually driving into the playground in order to collect/leave children. Although the drop off/pick up point is designated as the area beside the football area, this is in a very bad state and parents are reluctant to allow their children to cross over it.

It was decided that Mrs Rae would write to Dr Smith, at the Education Department, pointing out the Committee's concern and requesting that this area be maintained to a reasonable standard.

8   PLAY AREA

It was reported that the "Red Ash" play area of the playground was particularly bad and required attention. The headmaster agreed to write requesting an inspection of the playground and for subsequent remedial treatment to be carried out. He also undertook to send out a reminder to the children that they should not play in this particular area until further notice.

PARENT/TEACHER ASSOCIATION

9   GYM ACTIVITIES

The subject of activities undertaken in the gym period (ie running) being too strenuous for the children was raised. It was pointed out that this was not the policy of the gym teacher but rather of education in general. It is thought that children today are not fit enough due to general lack of exercise and the programme is designed to commence with a gradual build-up to 2 minutes running .

10   SPRING FAYRE

The date of Saturday, 27 May was set for the Spring Fayre and this will be notified to parents in the next Newsletter and discussed further at the next meeting.

11   NEXT MEETING

The next meeting of the Parent/Teacher Association will be held on Wednesday, 26 April 19__ at 1930 hours in the Senior School Staff Room.

Chairperson _ _ _ _ _ _ _ _ _ _ _ _ _ _ _ _ _

Date   _ _ _ _ _ _ _ _ _ _ _ _ _ _ _

4

Type the following text in a word processing package; then place it in a Desk Top Publishing file in Helvetica 10 pt text or similar. Create two columns using a 10 mm wide column guide and setting out the text as instructed. Save the document as DTP9 and print it.

THE JUSTICE SYSTEM ← *Stretch this text across both columns and centre it. Put in 20 pt bold text. Draw a rounded corner 4 pt line box around it out to the margins.*

Set an indent at 0.5 cm

1   On 17th May 1990 the European Court of Justice held that a pension paid under a contracted-out occupational pension scheme fell within the scope of Article 119 of the Treaty of Rome which requires equal pay for work of equal value. Prior to that time it was thought that pension benefits did not come within the definition of 'pay'.

2   The full legal implications of the case are unfortunately not conclusive. Areas of consensus centre on instalments of pensions received before 17th May 1990 (no problem, unless the employee had already made a legal claim) and secondly, on future pension accruals, which must be equalised for men and women doing jobs of equal value.

3   The concept of Article 119 seems to be related solely to the employer and employee relationship. There is, however, a minority legal view prevailing that because of the employer-trustee relationship in overall benefit provision, the trustees of the pension scheme are also required to ensure equalisation.

From here, put text in the second column. Remember to line up the first line of text in both columns.

After buying out the problem short-term, the UK Government would hopefully make a decision on the position of state pension age. You would then be in a much stronger position to amend the scheme on a basis consistent with the state and other occupational pension schemes.

At the very least, we would like to stress the importance of tackling matters for new starts, and ensure your awareness of the potential problem for existing members. The ultimate decision may, of course, have cost implications for the scheme which will be, to a greater or lesser extent, 'public' via SSAP24 and Social Security Act Disclosure Regulations.

We hope these guidelines are useful to you and your employees and would be grateful if you could return your comments to us at your own convenience.

Reopen DTP7 and make the following changes. Save the document as DTP9-1 and print a copy.

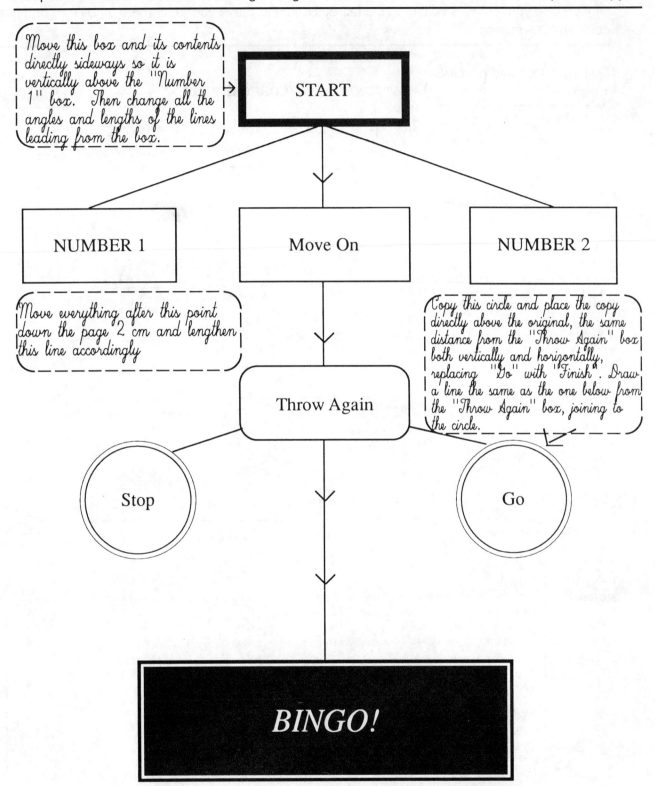

Move this box and its contents directly sideways so it is vertically above the "Number 1" box. Then change all the angles and lengths of the lines leading from the box.

START

NUMBER 1

Move On

NUMBER 2

Move everything after this point down the page 2 cm and lengthen this line accordingly

Copy this circle and place the copy directly above the original, the same distance from the "Throw Again" box both vertically and horizontally, replacing "Go" with "Finish". Draw a line the same as the one below from the "Throw Again" box, joining to the circle.

Throw Again

Stop

Go

BINGO!

Open a new file in Landscape mode and enter in the following text, using Helvetica 14 pt text or similar. Use your own discretion on the tab settings, etc. Save your document as DTP10 and print a copy on 70% scaling.

Centre, 20 pt bold, Helvetica or similar. → **NATIONAL CAR CORPORATION** ← *10 pt shaded box out to margins. 6 pt line around.*

Projected Returns For the Next 20 years

(Figures are in £m)

Put January to November all on the same line.

	Jan	Feb	Mar	Apr	May
Year 1	8,344	8,383	9,344	10,783	10,383
Year 2	9,787	10,049	9,787	11,346	11,049
Year 3	10,456	10,939	9,456	14,452	14,939
Year 4	12,784	14,994	12,784	16,384	16,994
Year 5	16,457	16,655	14,457	18,022	18,655
Year 6	18,567	18,744	16,567	20,737	20,744
Year 7	19,097	20,737	18,097	21,844	21,737
Year 8	22,747	22,999	21,747	23,787	23,999
Year 9	25,469	25,599	24,469	26,456	26,599
Year 10	30,783	30,193	26,783	29,838	29,193
Year 11	34,346	34,949	30,346	35,784	35,949
Year 12	46,452	49,893	51,452	52,457	52,893
Year 13	55,384	55,834	56,384	56,567	56,834
Year 14	65,022	70,838	70,022	74,097	74,838
Year 15	75,737	75,838	75,737	80,747	80,838
Year 16	78,766	78,677	78,766	84,469	84,677
Year 17	84,786	84,187	81,786	86,766	86,187
Year 18	86,879	84,948	82,879	90,786	90,948
Year 19	89,535	89,039	83,535	93,879	93,039
Year 20	94,838	94,839	96,838	99,535	99,839

Move this section

Jun	Jul	Aug	Sept	Oct	Nov
8,655	8,783	7,909	8,567	8,744	9,567
10,744	9,346	8,678	10,787	9,049	9,787
10,677	10,452	9,456	10,344	10,383	9,344
14,187	12,384	10,242	14,346	12,949	12,346
16,948	16,022	10,553	16,452	16,893	14,452
18,039	18,737	10,264	18,384	18,834	16,384
20,839	19,844	10,374	20,022	19,838	18,022
22,383	22,787	12,595	22,737	22,838	21,737
25,049	25,456	14,531	25,457	25,655	24,457
30,893	30,838	15,348	30,747	30,999	26,747
34,834	34,784	17,634	34,097	34,737	30,097
49,838	46,457	18,236	49,456	46,939	51,456
55,838	55,567	22,236	55,784	55,994	56,784
70,737	65,097	44,253	70,469	65,599	70,469
75,999	75,747	46,945	75,783	75,193	75,783
78,599	78,469	54,456	78,766	78,677	78,766
84,193	84,766	68,858	84,786	84,187	81,786
84,949	86,786	75,782	84,879	86,948	82,879
89,939	89,879	83,238	89,535	89,039	83,535
94,994	94,535	96,234	94,838	94,839	96,838

* Please note: Figures are not available for December

Put the table in a box with a 2 pt line. Separate the headings from the rest with a 2 pt horizontal line and separate each column with a 1 pt vertical line.

Reopen DTP10 and print a thumbnail copy.

Desk Top Publishing Exercise 11

Produce the following notice using appropriate clipart if it is available to you.

Are You As Fit As You Would Like To Think You Are?

Healthy eating and regular exercise should play a big part in everyone's life. Come along to the new weekly classes and we will give you new and exciting ideas in our exercise class (lasting approximately one hour) together with information on how to improve the eating habits of you and your family.

Meet new friends and share ideas with the class. Our instructors are all fully trained and will be on hand to give you all the help you need.

If this sounds good to you come along to:

If you have Clipart available place something appropriate to exercise here, cropping if necessary

The Smith Hall,
Scott Street,
Stringtoun.

at 7.30 on Tuesday.

If you have Clipart available place something concerning food here, cropping if necessary

Remember to bring Jogging Trousers, etc, for the exercise class.

Shower facilities are available.

Enter the following in a word processing package and place into a new desk top publishing file. Recreate it as follows. Save as DTP12 and print a copy. Use appropriate cliparts if they are available to you.

Social Groups in France - 1789 to 1793

To a certain extent the demands of different social groups in France between 1789 and 1793 were met. The ideas of Liberalism and the Enlightenment had won through, but there was still much discontent, especially among the urban workers.

The peasants were the main benefactors after the French Revolution. They had ownership of their land. More land was available because of the selling of church land and this quelled any unrest about land shortages. Before the Revolution peasants had to pay a considerable amount of money on taxes and seignorial dues. For example, about 8% of their income went to the church and they had to make cash payments to the seignior to commute their obligations. After the Revolution, however, these dues were not paid and taxes were at a better level. The peasant, who could not feed himself before, was now encouraged to sell grain for profit and feed himself. The peasants therefore benefited greatly after 1789.

The ideas of the Enlightenment that sparked off the Revolution were put forward by the up and coming merchant class. The idea that property was nearly sacred (ownership of property gave you independence from control) and that Market Forces should be used to determine economics and not government intervention appealed to the rising bourgeoisie. After 1789 these demands were met, almost entirely.

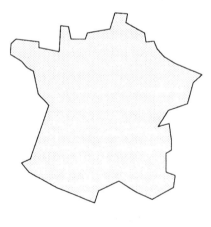

Guild restrictions were abolished. These were seen by merchants to be a barrier to the expansion of industry, because they kept the numbers in the guild under control, so that output was small, but good quality. Tariff barriers were pulled down, another obstacle to trade eliminated. The bourgeoisie also was able to buy its way into government and, in the case of the very rich, into a hereditary nobility. The rise in the status of this new class and the fact trade was now under its control meant that its demands on the whole were met. Bankers became especially strong because everybody, even the King, needed to borrow money (this placed them under the bankers' control).

The most dissatisfied group after 1789 must have been the urban workers, especially the artisans. Their position had only slightly changed after 1789. They saw the Liberal Revolution as not going far enough. The grain harvest failure and subsequent rise in the price of bread meant that in some cases 4/5ths of earnings was going on the staple diet.

The urban craftsmen had seen their guilds disposed of and the emergence of a large semi-skilled workforce. They saw their position as being threatened. The fear of starvation therefore lead the urban mass to rebel and seize grain. They were not shot because the reformists in power saw the solution used by an absolutist monarchy. In any case, to increase the army you had to be the monarch and the aim was less, not more power for the King. The solution was therefore appeasement. Shrewd politicians now saw the force of the urban mass and used it to swing political meetings. The emergence of the Sans Culotte at this time was very significant.

The flight of the King in 1791 dashed all hopes of a liberal reforming monarchy. The Jacobins, committed revolutionaries, supported by the Sans Culotte, urban workers, called for a Republic and the abdication of the King. The influence and support of this left wing movement grew after the

defeat of France by Austria. It was hoped the war would unite France and let the government lock up any opponents for treason, etc. In fact, the war brought defeat and economic ruin to France. The Sans Culotte and Jacobins eventually gained power and the guilds were brought back. France was relatively prosperous in this period but eventually crumbled after the initial re-emergence fell under heavy criticism.

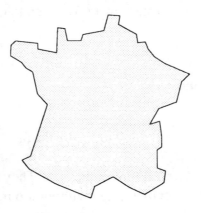

The artisans and the peasants both looked backwards in time for a settlement, not forward. The artisans wanted guild

restrictions and a minimum wage and maximum price for bread, not Market Forces. The peasants wanted land and the strength of agriculture, not industrial developments. To an extent these demands were met eventually. Farming stayed virtually the same archaic system as before.

A word must be said about the aristocrats in this period. Some aligned themselves to the ideas of the Enlightenment and fully supported the Revolution. Most, however, fled France and perpetually tried to undermine her position under the Liberal Constitution. These Emigres, as they were called, raised armies and supported foreign attempts to bring down France.

Some social groups therefore did gain what they wanted in the period 1789-1793. The peasants gained all they wanted and the liberals were in government. The urban workers, however, were left dissatisfied, until they seized power later on.

The End

Desk top publishing solutions

Desk Top Publishing Exercise 1

Desk Top Publishing can be a very powerful tool to the user. It enables even a novice to create effective, professional-looking documentation without too much effort.

A document which is pleasing to the eye will entice a reader more than just columns of text, and splitting text using simple tools like lines and boxes will undoubtedly make the reader keener to look at the information you are trying to convey.

It is well known that people read VDU monitors less accurately than printed pages. Moreover, the VDU is unable to show artwork as effectively as the printed page. Producing a draft copy of your document before you decide on the final layout is a wise idea. This enables you to check each page individually and also to check the entire documentation for any errors which you may not have noticed onscreen.

Remember, save your documentation often. If you make a change which you decide you don't like or do something drastically wrong, then you can easily go back to one of your previous versions without having to start again from scratch.

Desk Top Publishing Exercise 1.1

Desk Top Publishing

DTP Packages can be a very powerful tool to the user. They enable even a novice to create effective, professional-looking documentation without too much time and effort.

A document which is pleasing to the eye will entice a reader more than just columns of text, and splitting text using simple tools like lines and boxes will make the reader keener to look at the information you are trying to convey.

It is a well known fact that people read VDU monitors less accurately than printed pages. Moreover, the VDU is unable to show artwork as effectively as the printed page. Producing a draft copy of your document before you decide on the final layout is a wise idea. This enables you to check each page individually and also to check the entire documentation for any errors which you may not have noticed onscreen.

Don't forget to save your documentation often. If you make a change which you decide you don't like or do something silly, then you can easily go back to one of your previous versions without having to start again from scratch.

Desk Top Publishing Exercise 2

If you have never used a word processing package, there are a few simple rules which you should follow.

Firstly, you should always name your documents according to the information which they contain. There is nothing worse than trying to locate a file months later when you cannot remember what you called it.

Secondly, you should always proofread everything prior to saving and printing. Of invaluable assistance is the spell check facility. Using this feature, the program loads the UK English dictionary and proceeds to check your spelling throughout the entire document. Unfortunately, it also picks out proper names and technical information which the dictionary does not contain.

Lastly, never erase anything without considering carefully whether or not you really want to do this. Imagine a whole day's work wasted because of one mistake!

Desk Top Publishing Exercise 2.1

If you have never used a word processing package, there are a few simple rules which you should follow.

Firstly,

you should always name your documents according to the information which they contain. There is nothing worse than trying to locate a file months later when you cannot remember what you called it.

Secondly,

you should always proofread everything prior to saving and printing. Of invaluable assistance is the spell check facility. Using this feature, the program loads the UK English dictionary and proceeds to check your spelling throughout the entire document. Unfortunately, it also picks out proper names and technical information which the dictionary does not contain.

Lastly,

never erase anything without considering carefully whether or not you really want to do this. Imagine a whole day's work wasted because of one mistake!

Animal Passion Fashion

This year the clothes are being created to bring out the beast in you...

Now various different animal effect patterns available in Lycra are appearing in High Street shops more and more frequently. The range includes snake, tiger and zebra and they will be all the rage as you prowl around. The designers are trying to put a little fun into fashion this year and due to the recession they are also trying to keep the prices down.

Accessories are an integral part of fashion, and you can easily update last year's clothes or that sale bargain with a change of buttons, the addition of a scarf or wrap, and the judicious use of a piece of jewellery.

The accessory that makes your outfit come alive can often give an individual aura to your dress sense.

The fact is that fashion accessories from belts to boots and bags are an inexpensive way of extending the life of your existing wardrobe.

Florals and pastels are still very popular for most but the more daring amongst us will soon be dazzling everyone in these new fabrics. Lycra looks stunning ... if you have a model figure, but unfortunately, for most of us it stretches out of recognition with our bulges!

Don't despair, though. There are always ways of wearing clothes to suit your particular figure. Fashion these days is all about adapting outfits to suit yourself.

So don't be a fashion victim... look at what's available and then choose an outfit that will fit your figure best.

Desk Top Publishing

DTP Packages can be a very powerful tool to the user. They enable even a novice to create effective, professional-looking documentation without too much time and effort.

A document which is pleasing to the eye will entice a reader more than just columns of text, and splitting text using simple tools like lines and boxes will make the reader keener to look at the information you are trying to convey.

It is well known that people read VDU monitors less accurately than printed pages. Moreover, the VDU is unable to show artwork as effectively as the printed page. Producing a draft copy of your document before you decide on the final layout is a wise idea. This enables you to check each page individually and also to check the entire documentation for any errors which you may not have noticed onscreen.

Don't forget to save your documentation often. If you make a change which you decide you don't like or do something silly, then you can easily go back to one of your previous versions without having to start again from scratch.

■ ■

Desk Top Publishing

DTP Packages can be a very powerful tool to the user. They enable even a novice to create effective, professional-looking documentation without too much time and effort.

A document which is pleasing to the eye will entice a reader more than just columns of text, and splitting text using simple tools like lines and boxes will make the reader keener to look at the information you are trying to convey.

It is well known that people read VDU monitors less accurately than printed pages. Moreover, the VDU is unable to show artwork as effectively as the printed page. Producing a draft copy of your document before you decide on the final layout is a wise idea. This enables you to check each page individually and also to check the entire documentation for any errors which you may not have noticed onscreen.

Don't forget to save your documentation often. If you make a change which you decide you don't like or do something silly, then you can easily go back to one of your previous versions without having to start again from scratch.

HIGHER/VOCATIONAL EDUCATION COMMITTEE
Certificate

The teaching of this certificate should be approached from the standpoint of the supervisor - a student-centred learning approach. This may be achieved by allowing the student to gain hands-on experience of a desk top publishing program progressively, with the tutor demonstrating new material and good working practice.

The collecting of samples produced by software houses, eg books/manuals, could usefully be employed to help build an appreciation of design principles. Opportunities should be provided regularly for group discussions, particularly for the more aesthetic components of desk top publishing, and discussions on artistic qualities should be encouraged.

The use of audio-visual aids, together with visits to printers or design studios, could be incorporated and group work, where students explore the uses and problems of incorporating a desk top publishing program, is recommended.

Acceptable performance will be satisfactory achievement of all aspects of the study area and the exact requirements of each section are clearly detailed in the summary sheet which has been issued to all centres.

Please note

The above notes are only rough guidelines and do not have to be carried out verbatim.

Desk Top Publishing can be a very powerful tool to the user. It enables even a novice to create effective, professional-looking documentation without too much effort.

A document which is pleasing to the eye will entice a reader more than just columns of text, and splitting text using simple tools like lines and boxes will undoubtedly make the reader keener to look at the information you are trying to convey.

It is well known that people read VDU monitors less accurately than printed pages. Moreover, the VDU is unable to show artwork as effectively as the printed page. Producing a draft copy of your document before you decide on the final layout is a wise idea. This enables you to check each page individually and also to check the entire documentation for any errors which you may not have noticed onscreen.

Remember, save your documentation often. If you make a change which you decide you don't like or do something drastically wrong, then you can easily go back to one of your previous versions without having to start again from scratch.

———————————————
———————————————

Desk Top Publishing can be a very powerful tool to the user. It enables even a novice to create effective, professional-looking documentation without too much effort.

———————————————
———————————————

A document which is pleasing to the eye will entice a reader more than just columns of text, and splitting text using simple tools like lines and boxes will undoubtedly make the reader keener to look at the information you are trying to convey.

———————————————
———————————————

It is well known that people read VDU monitors less accurately than printed pages. Moreover, the VDU is unable to show artwork as effectively as the printed page. Producing a draft copy of your document before you decide on the final layout is a wise idea. This enables you to check each page individually and also to check the entire documentation for any errors which you may not have noticed onscreen.

———————————————
———————————————

Remember, save your documentation often. If you make a change which you decide you don't like or do something drastically wrong, then you can easily go back to one of your previous versions without having to start again from scratch.

———————————————
———————————————

SENIOR CITIZEN FARES

	26 Dec-13 May 14 Oct-14 Dec		14 May-08 Jul 17 Sept-14 Oct		09 Jul-16 Sept 15 Dec-25 Dec	
TO	London	Glasgow	London	Glasgow	London	Glasgow
St Johns	369.00	-	410.57	-	461.00	-
Halifax	369.00	369.00	410.00	410.00	461.00	461.00
Gander	369.00	349.00	410.00	410.00	461.00	-
Montreal	369.00	-	410.00	-	461.00	-
Vancouver	503.50	503.50	544.00	544.00	585.50	585.50
Edmonton	482.00	-	523.00	-	564.00	-

Special Offer

Glasgow/London (Return)	99.00	99.00	109.00	109.00	125.00	125.00

(Excluding Monday/Friday flights when full fare will be applied)

COMPUTER PROGRAMS

Word Processing is a computer program which allows you to enter and edit text. Anything which would be done on a typewriter can normally be entered into a word processing program. Even good typists make mistakes, but by using a word processing program you can have perfect copies every time. You can even check your spelling so there is no need to worry about documents being sent out with errors.

There is really no need to worry about using a word processing program and most people who have been reluctant to use one in the first instance would never be without one now. A word processing program will usually make what is called a .BAK file so, if you do get into difficulties, you always have your 'back-up' file to save the day.

(second page)

COMPUTER PROGRAMS

A Desk Top Publishing system enables the user to produce documents to a professional standard. You may enter and edit text, use bold, italic and underline, and practically every other function available in a word processing package.

Desk Top Publishing, however, lets you go a step further, by allowing you to change font styles and sizes, add lines, shaded boxes and circles, and even bring in graphics from other packages. Thus, Desk Top Publishing allows you to produce an impressive document quickly and easily. Even a novice can create effective and professional-looking publications.

COMPUTER PROGRAMS

a)   Word Processing is a computer program which allows you to enter and edit text. Anything which would be done on a typewriter can normally be entered into a word processing program. Even good typists make mistakes, but by using a word processing program you can have perfect copies every time. You can even check your spelling so there is no need to worry about documents being sent out with errors.

b)   There is really no need to worry about using a word processing program and most people who have been reluctant to use one in the first instance would never be without one now. A word processing program will usually make what is called a .BAK file so, if you do get into difficulties, you always have your 'back-up' file to save the day.

1

COMPUTER PROGRAMS

c)   A Desk Top Publishing system enables the user to produce documents to a
     professional standard. You may enter and edit text, use bold, italic and underline,
     and practically every other function available in a word processing package.

d)   Desk Top Publishing, however, lets you go a step further, by allowing you to
     change font styles and sizes, add lines, shaded boxes and circles, and even bring
     in graphics from other packages. Thus, Desk Top Publishing allows you to
     produce an impressive document quickly and easily. Even a novice can create
     effective and professional-looking publications.

2

ROYAL PRESERVATION FUND

Regional Examination Results

	Number of students	Average % gained this year	Average % gained over last 10 years
Cleveland	200	51.5	65
Greater Manchester	71	83.0	85
Lothian	158	74.6	86
Gwynedd	499	60.0	63
Inner London	1,333	46.9	49
Strathclyde	981	39.0	49
Manchester	5	98.3	93

These results show that students in most areas have gained slightly lower results than in previous years.

On more careful examination of the table we can deduce that students sitting exams in areas where the Preservation Fund exams are less popular tend to have a higher pass rate.

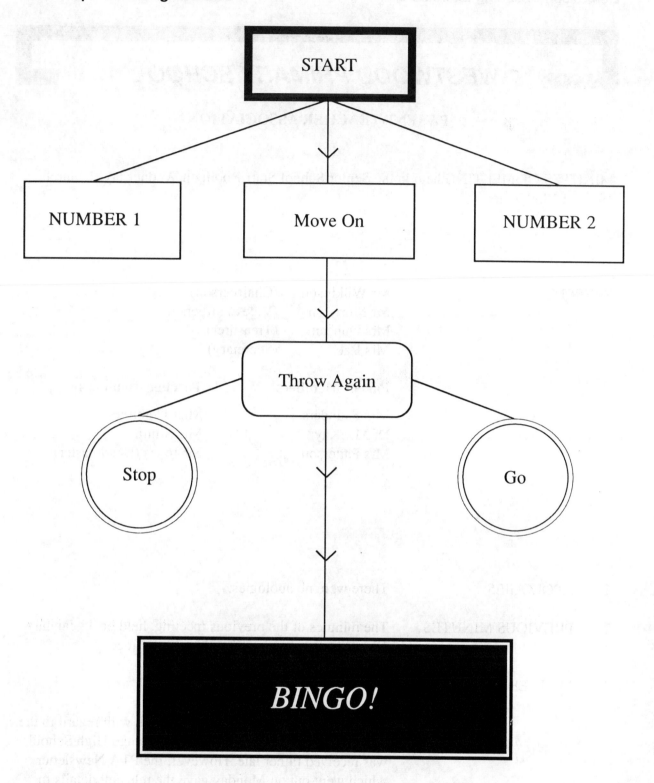

WESTWOOD PRIMARY SCHOOL

PARENT/TEACHER ASSOCIATION

MINUTES OF MEETING held in the Senior School Staff Room on Wednesday, 1 March 19__ at 1930 hours.

PRESENT		
	Mr Wilkinson	(Chairperson)
	Mr Morrison	(Vice Chairperson)
	Mrs Duncan	(Treasurer)
	Mrs Rae	(Secretary)

Parent Members	**Teacher Members**
Mrs Saunders	Miss Crabtree
Dr MacKay	Mrs Smith
Mrs Patterson	Mr Jones (Headmaster)

1	APOLOGIES	There were no apologies.
2	PREVIOUS MINUTES	The minutes of the previous meeting, held on 11 January 19__ were read and accepted by Committee.
3	MATTERS ARISING	**3.1 SCHOOL BOARDS**

Mr Wilkinson reported that notification with regard to the School Board meeting to be held at Grange High School was received rather late. However, the PTA Newsletter which went out on Monday gave the relevant details to parents.

1

PARENT/TEACHER ASSOCIATION

Mrs Rae reported that notification with regard to a meeting to be held in Rivers Primary School on 14 February was also received too late and that she had written to the Secretary of the PTF requesting that all future correspondence be sent directly to the school and pointing out that the late arrival was the reason for no PTA members being present from the school. A copy of the Minutes of the Meeting was also requested for perusal by the Committee.

Mr Wilkinson also reported that he had received notification that about 80 parents would attend the meeting at the local high school on Tuesday, 7 March.

It was agreed that the Video would be shown at the next Committee meeting and that this would take priority on the Agenda.

3.2 PLAYING FIELDS

Mr Wilkinson read letters which he had received from Mr Roberts of the LEC and Mr Crawford, MP (together with copies of correspondence received from the Education Department) with regard to the proposed playing fields.

The matter of making application to the European Social Fund was also discussed and it was decided that the Committee would await further correspondence from the LEC and Donald Crawford before making any approach to the ESF.

4 SOCIAL EVENT

Mr Wilkinson reported that approximately 100 attendees were expected and that arrangements for the supply of wine and glasses had been made, and Mrs Duncan and Mrs Saunders had the food supplies under control.

Mr Jones will purchase all the necessary supplies from the Cash & Carry.

Mr Morrison gave a demonstration of how the 'Race Night' activities would be operated and Mrs Smith volunteered to sell tickets (20p each). It was agreed that the proceeds from one of the races would be donated to "Comic Relief".

PARENT/TEACHER ASSOCIATION

5   SCHOOL BUS

5.1 Mr Wilkinson said that 25 parents had indicated an interest in running a bus from the west side to/from the school and the headmaster agreed to obtain names of children in this area from the class lists in order that further correspondence may be directed accordingly.

5.2 Mr Wilkinson also reported that he had been approached with regard to a similar service being available to/from the top end of town and it was agreed that a tear-off slip would be included on the next Newsletter requesting an indication of interest.

6   FOOTBALL AREA

The matter of dogs fouling the footpath and play area was brought to the attention of the Committee. It was agreed that the Secretary would write, in the first instance, to the Director of the Environment indicating the Committee's concern and requesting appropriate action.

7   CAR PARKING

It was brought to the attention of the Committee that there was, once again, a problem with regard to cars parking too near to the school crossing areas, coupled with the additional problem of parents or guardians actually driving into the playground in order to collect/leave children. Although the drop off/pick up point is designated as the area beside the football area, this is in a very bad state and parents are reluctant to allow their children to cross over it.

It was decided that Mrs Rae would write to Dr Smith, at the Education Department, pointing out the Committee's concern and requesting that this area be maintained to a reasonable standard.

8   PLAY AREA

It was reported that the 'Red Ash' play area of the playground was particularly bad and required attention. The headmaster agreed to write requesting an inspection of the playground and for subsequent remedial treatment to be carried out. He also undertook to send out a reminder to the children that they should not play in this particular area until further notice.

3

PARENT/TEACHER ASSOCIATION

9   GYM ACTIVITIES

The subject of activities undertaken in the gym period (ie running) being too strenuous for the children was raised. It was pointed out that this was not the policy of the gym teacher but rather of education in general. It is thought that children today are not fit enough due to general lack of exercise and the programme is designed to commence with a gradual build-up to 2 minutes running.

10   SPRING FAYRE

The date of Saturday, 27 May was set for the Spring Fayre and this will be notified to parents in the next Newsletter and discussed further at the next meeting.

11   NEXT MEETING

The next meeting of the Parent/Teacher Association will be held on Wednesday, 26 April 19__ at 1930 hours in the Senior School Staff Room.

Chairperson _ _ _ _ _ _ _ _ _ _ _ _ _ _ _ _ _

Date _ _ _ _ _ _ _ _ _ _ _ _ _ _ _ _ _

4

THE JUSTICE SYSTEM

1 On 17th May 1990 the European Court of Justice held that a pension paid under a contracted-out occupational pension scheme fell within the scope of Article 119 of the Treaty of Rome which requires equal pay for work of equal value. Prior to that time it was thought that pension benefits did not come within the definition of 'pay'.

2 The full legal implications of the case are unfortunately not conclusive. Areas of consensus centre on instalments of pensions received before 17th May 1990 (no problem, unless the employee had already made a legal claim) and secondly, on future pension accruals, which must be equalised for men and women doing jobs of equal value.

3 The concept of Article 119 seems to be related solely to the employer and employee relationship. There is, however, a minority legal view prevailing that because of the employer-trustee relationship in overall benefit provision, the trustees of the pension scheme are also required to ensure equalisation.

After buying out the problem short-term, the UK Government would hopefully make a decision on the position of state pension age. You would then be in a much stronger position to amend the scheme on a basis consistent with the state and other occupational pension schemes.

At the very least, we would like to stress the importance of tackling matters for new starts, and ensure your awareness of the potential problem for existing members. The ultimate decision may, of course, have cost implications for the scheme which will be, to a greater or lesser extent, 'public' via SSAP24 and Social Security Act Disclosure Regulations.

We hope these guidelines are useful to you and your employees and would be grateful if you could return your comments to us at your own convenience.

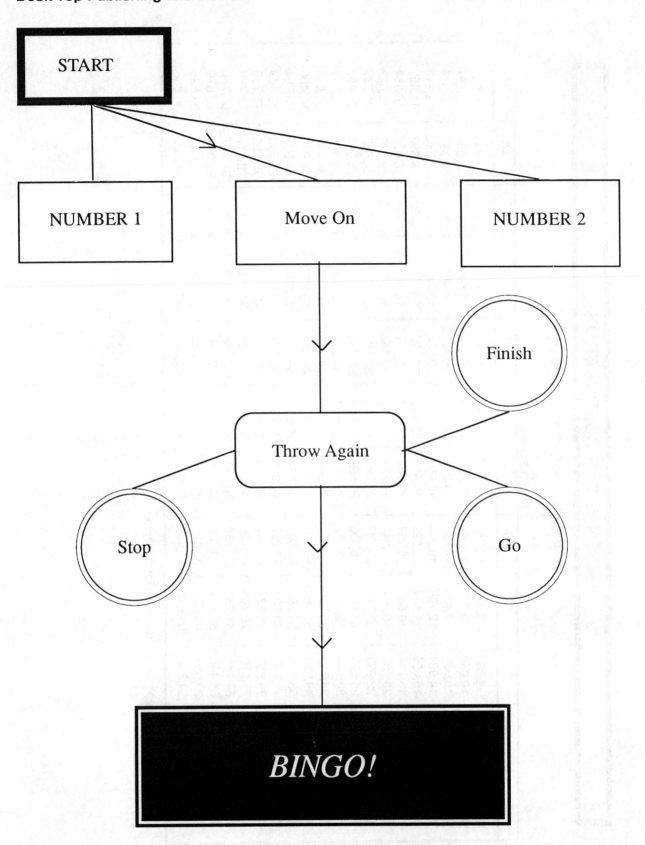

NATIONAL CAR CORPORATION

Projected Returns For the Next 20 years

(Figures are in £m)

	Jan	Feb	Mar	Apr	May	Jun	Jul	Aug	Sept	Oct	Nov
Year 1	8,344	8,383	9,344	10,783	10,383	8,655	8,783	7,909	8,567	8,744	9,567
Year 2	9,787	10,049	9,787	11,346	11,049	10,744	9,346	8,678	10,787	9,049	9,787
Year 3	10,456	10,939	9,456	14,452	14,939	10,677	10,452	9,456	10,344	10,383	9,344
Year 4	12,784	14,994	12,784	16,384	16,994	14,187	12,384	10,242	14,346	12,949	12,346
Year 5	16,457	16,655	14,457	18,022	18,655	16,948	16,022	10,553	16,452	16,893	14,452
Year 6	18,567	18,744	16,567	20,737	20,744	18,039	18,737	10,264	18,384	18,834	16,384
Year 7	19,097	20,737	18,097	21,844	21,737	20,839	19,844	10,374	20,022	19,838	18,022
Year 8	22,747	22,999	21,747	23,787	23,999	22,383	22,787	12,595	22,737	22,838	21,737
Year 9	25,469	25,599	24,469	26,456	26,599	25,049	25,456	14,531	25,457	25,655	24,457
Year 10	30,783	30,193	26,783	29,838	29,193	30,893	30,838	15,348	30,747	30,999	26,747
Year 11	34,346	34,949	30,346	35,784	35,949	34,834	34,784	17,634	34,097	34,737	30,097
Year 12	46,452	49,893	51,452	52,457	52,893	49,838	46,457	18,236	49,456	46,939	51,456
Year 13	55,384	55,834	56,384	56,567	56,834	55,838	55,567	22,236	55,784	55,994	56,784
Year 14	65,022	70,838	70,022	74,097	74,838	70,737	65,097	44,253	70,469	65,599	70,469
Year 15	75,737	75,838	75,737	80,747	80,838	75,999	75,747	46,945	75,783	75,193	75,783
Year 16	78,766	78,677	78,766	84,469	84,677	78,599	78,469	54,456	78,766	78,677	78,766
Year 17	84,786	84,187	81,786	86,766	86,187	84,193	84,766	68,858	84,786	84,187	81,786
Year 18	86,879	84,948	82,879	90,786	90,948	84,949	86,786	75,782	84,879	86,948	82,879
Year 19	89,535	89,039	83,535	93,879	93,039	89,939	89,879	83,238	89,535	89,039	83,535
Year 20	94,838	94,839	96,838	99,535	99,839	94,994	94,535	96,234	94,838	94,839	96,838

* Please note: Figures are not available for December

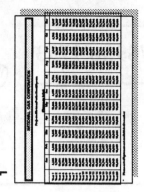

Are You As Fit As You Would Like To Think You Are?

Healthy eating and regular exercise should play a big part in everyone's life. Come along to the new weekly classes and we will give you new and exciting ideas in our exercise class (lasting approximately one hour) together with information on how to improve the eating habits of you and your family.

Meet new friends and share ideas with the class. Our instructors are all fully trained and will be on hand to give you all the help you need.

If this sounds good to you come along to:

The Smith Hall,
Scott Street,
Stringtoun.

at 7.30 on Tuesday.

Remember to bring Jogging Trousers, etc, for the exercise class.

Shower facilities are available.

Social Groups in France - 1789 to 1793

To a certain extent the demands of different social groups in France between 1789 and 1793 were met. The ideas of Liberalism and the Enlightenment had won through, but there was still much discontent, especially among the urban workers.

The peasants were the main benefactors after the French Revolution. They had ownership of their land. More land was available because of the selling of church land and this quelled any unrest about land shortages. Before the Revolution peasants had to pay a considerable amount of money on taxes and seignorial dues. For example, about 8% of their income went to the church and they had to make cash payments to the seignior to commute their obligations. After the Revolution, however, these dues were not paid and taxes were at a better level. The peasant, who could not feed himself before, was now encouraged to sell grain for profit and feed himself. The peasants therefore benefited greatly after 1789.

The ideas of the Enlightenment that sparked off the Revolution were put forward by the up and coming merchant class. The idea that property was nearly sacred (ownership of property gave you independence from control) and that Market Forces should be used to determine economics and not government intervention appealed to the rising bourgeoisie. After 1789 these demands were met, almost entirely.

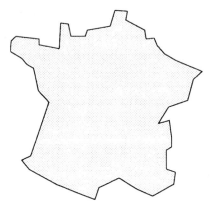

Guild restrictions were abolished. These were seen by merchants to be a barrier to the expansion of industry, because they kept the numbers in the guild under control, so that output was small, but good quality. Tariff barriers were pulled down, another obstacle to trade eliminated. The bourgeoisie also was able to buy its way into government and, in the case of the very rich, into a hereditary nobility. The rise in the status of this new class and the fact trade was now under its control meant that its demands on the whole were met. Bankers became especially strong because everybody, even the King, needed to borrow money (this placed them under the bankers' control).

The most dissatisfied group after 1789 must have been the urban workers, especially the artisans. Their position had only slightly changed after 1789. They saw the Liberal Revolution as not going far enough. The grain harvest failure and subsequent rise in the price of bread meant that in some cases 4/5ths of earnings was going on the staple diet.

The urban craftsmen had seen their guilds disposed of and the emergence of a large semi-skilled workforce. They saw their position as being threatened. The fear of starvation therefore lead the urban mass to rebel and seize grain. They were not shot because the reformists in power saw that means as being the solution used by an absolutist monarchy. In any case, to increase the army you had to be the monarch and the aim was less, not more power for the King. The solution was therefore appeasement. Shrewd politicians now saw the force of the urban mass and used it to swing political meetings. The emergence of the Sans Culotte at this time was very significant.

The flight of the King in 1791 dashed all hopes of a liberal reforming monarchy. The Jacobins, committed revolutionaries, supported by the Sans Culotte, urban workers, called for a Republic and the abdication of the King. The influence and support of this left wing movement grew after the defeat of France by Austria. It was hoped the war would unite France and let the government lock up any opponents for treason, etc. In fact, the war brought defeat and economic ruin to France. The Sans Culotte and Jacobins eventually gained power and the guilds were brought back. France was relatively prosperous in this period but eventually crumbled after the initial re-emergence fell under heavy criticism.

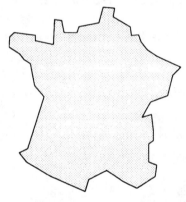

The artisans and the peasants both looked backwards in time for a settlement, not forward. The artisans wanted guild restrictions and a minimum wage and maximum price for bread, not Market Forces. The peasants wanted land and the strength of agriculture, not industrial developments. To an extent these demands were met eventually. Farming stayed virtually the same archaic system as before.

A word must be said about the aristocrats in this period. Some aligned themselves to the ideas of the Enlightenment and fully supported the Revolution. Most, however, fled France and perpetually tried to undermine her position under the Liberal Constitution. These Emigres, as they were called, raised armies and supported foreign attempts to bring down France.

Some social groups therefore did gain what they wanted in the period 1789-1793. The peasants gained all they wanted and the liberals were in government. The urban workers, however, were left dissatisfied, until they seized power later on.

The End

Spreadsheet exercises

What is a spreadsheet program?

A spreadsheet is a calculations program. Any task that could be carried out using a calculator and paper may be done more efficiently on a computer by using a spreadsheet package. Once data has been input and stored, it may be retrieved and changed, with automatic recalculation of all the relevant figures. Therefore, a spreadsheet program is very suitable for routine tasks which require continuous recalculation of figures.

Uses of spreadsheet packages

Balance Sheets · Sales Records · Cashflow Analysis

Any tasks which normally involve calculations of any kind can be performed by a spreadsheet program. You are limited only by the program which you are using.

Examples of spreadsheet packages

SuperCalc · Lotus 1-2-3 · CalcStar · PC Planner

Basically, a spreadsheet looks like the example shown here:

Rows	Labels	Columns				
		A :	B :	C :	D :	E
1:		1ST Q	2ND Q	3RD Q	4TH Q	
2:	AREA 1	1200				
3:	AREA 2	1000				
4:	AREA 3	900				
5:	AREA 4	700				
		SUM (A2..A5) = Formula				

The spreadsheet, often referred to as a worksheet, is read according to the co-ordinates – like reading a map.

Each **unit**, eg column B row 2, column B row 3, is referred to as a **cell** and the highlight bar is the **cellpointer.**

You move around a spreadsheet using the arrow keys in the computer keyboard.

The cell address (eg column B row 2) and the cell contents will always be displayed on the status line, which will usually be either at the top or bottom of the screen.

Text entries are interpreted as **labels** and numerical entries as **values. Calculations are only carried out on values**.

Summary

A spreadsheet is an application program which allows you to carry out complicated calculations and cell/worksheet linking – ie when one figure is amended, all linked cells are recalculated.

Reading a spreadsheet

Look at the spreadsheet below and answer the following questions:

	A	B	C	D
1				
2	ITEM	JAN	FEB	MAR
3				
4	GENTS' SOCKS	500	300	200
5	LADIES' SOCKS	170	150	125
6	CHILDREN'S SOCKS	50	40	70
7				
8	TOTAL	720	490	395

1 Refer to cell A2. What does this cell contain?
   Is this a 'value' or a 'label'?
2 Refer to cell D6. What does it contain?
   Is this a 'value' or a 'label'?
3 What are the co-ordinates of the cell containing JAN?
4 What are the co-ordinates of the cell containing 125?
5 A range – from one cell location to another – is part of a spreadsheet. For example, A1.D6 would include all entries starting from cell A1 to cell D6 and B1.B8 would include all entries in column B above.

Summary of new commands used in each exercise

The following is a summary of the commands you will need to know before starting each exercise. Please check with your tutor or consult your software program manual for advice where necessary. Write the command sequences in your notebook for future use.

Exercise 1   Basic entering skills · Save and print skills · Clear screen command

Exercise 1.1   Recalling files · Using Data Fill · Formatting commands · Totalling columns · Adding and subtracting non-adjacent cells

Exercise 1.2   Global column-width · Local column-width · Editing cell contents

Exercise 2   Right-aligning labels · Entering combined labels

Exercise 2.1   Replacing cell contents · Totalling rows · Adding blank rows · Using Cell Fill

Exercise 2.2   Adding blank columns · Editing formulae · Printing specified ranges · Hiding ranges · Using the copy command · Printing with wide margins/reduced print

Exercise 2.3   Saving part of a worksheet · Erasing ranges

Exercise 3   Consolidation of previously used commands

Exercise 4   Absolute cell referencing · Using wider margins/reduced print · Freezing titles

Exercise 4.1   Sorting a column · Moving columns/ranges · Combining files · Erasing ranges

Exercise 5   Consolidation of previously used commands

Exercise 5.1   Consolidation of previously used commands

Exercise 5.2   Manual calculation · More complex formulae

Exercise 5.3   File combine

Exercise 5.4   Mathematical functions: Count
Max
Min
Avg

Exercise 6   Creating graphs

Exercise 7   Editing graphs

Exercise 8   Backing up your worksheets

Exercise 9   Intaking tables from text files · Calculating on text files

Exercise 9.1   Intaking and calculating tables from text files · Using IF function

Spreadsheet Exercise 1

Key in the following spreadsheet, entering the labels and numbers in the cells as shown.

	A	B	C	D	E	F	G
1	CHEQUE BOOK ACCOUNT – JANUARY						
2							
3				CHEQUE	DEPOSIT		
4	CHEQUE	DATE	DESCRPT	AMOUNT	AMOUNT	BALANCE	
5		Jan 03				1250	
6		Jan 08	Groceries	90			
7		Jan 10	Petrol	30			
8		Jan 12	Butcher	15			
9		Jan 13	Material	45			
10		Jan 13	Comm Chrg	65			
11		Jan 15	Groceries	45			
12		Jan 17	Butcher	12			
13		Jan 20	Elect	110			
14		Jan 20	Petrol	25			
15		Jan 21	Gas	80			
16		Jan 22	Groceries	25			
17		Jan 23	Credit	96			
18		Jan 25	B. Soc	360			
19		Jan 26	Insurance	56			
20		Jan 28	Car Insur	210			
21							
22		Jan 30	Salary		1015		

On completion, save and print your worksheet (using the filename EX1). Clear your screen, ready to commence Exercise 1.1.

Spreadsheet Exercise 1.1

Recall Exercise 1 and then make the following alterations:

1 Using the DATA FILL command, fill from A6 to A20 with cheque numbers, commencing with 10607 and finishing with 10621
2 Total all cheques in cell D21
3 In cell F21, subtract the total in D21 from the balance in cell F5
4 In cell F22, add the balance in cell F21 to the deposit amount in E22
5 Format all cells containing currency figures to display 2 decimal places
6 Take 2 printouts – one displaying formulae as text
7 Look at your printouts. Using your manual, can you establish why one printout shows asterisks instead of figures? Write your answer at the bottom of your printout
8 Prior to saving your worksheet as EX1.1., reset your cells to display values

Clear your screen prior to commencing Exercise 1.2.

Spreadsheet Exercise 1.2

Recall Exercise 1.1 and make the following alterations:

1 Using the Global format command, set the column widths to 8
2 Move to column C and set the current column width to 15
3 Using the **GOTO** key, move to cell C10 and edit the label to read **Comm Charge**
4 Using the **GOTO** key, move to cell C13 and edit the label to read **Electricity**
5 Move to cell E22 and format the contents to display zero (0) decimal places
6 Repeat step 5 at cell F5
7 Using the Global format command, set the column widths to 12
8 Take a printout of your modified worksheet and save it as EX1.2

Spreadsheet Exercise 2

Prepare the following spreadsheet for the monthly sales figures:

1 Using the format below, enter the labels: PRODUCT, JAN, FEB, MAR, in row 1
2 Enter the following labels down column A: 5¼" DISKS
                                               3½" DISKS
                                               A4 FORM FEED
                                               A4 CONTINUOUS
                                               A3 FORM FEED
                                               A3 CONTINUOUS
                                               CARBON RIBBONS
                                               FABRIC RIBBONS
3 Using the Global format command, set the range containing values so that these are displayed as fixed with zero decimal places

PRODUCT	JAN	FEB	MAR
5¼" DISKS	1500	1200	1300
3½" DISKS	1200	1350	1500
A4 FORM FEED	1050	1200	900
A4 CONTINUOUS	2000	2100	1950
A3 FORM FEED	900	700	1200
A3 CONTINUOUS	2500	2100	1900
CARBON RIBBONS	750	650	780
FABRIC RIBBONS	250	450	170

4 Set the Global column width to 14
5 Calculate the monthly totals
6 Right align all headings
7 On completion, print 2 copies of the spreadsheet – one displaying formulae as text.
8 Prior to saving your worksheet as EX2, reset your cells to display values

Clear your screen before commencing Exercise 2.1

Spreadsheet Exercise 2.1

Recall the file in Exercise 2 and make the following alterations to the worksheet:

1 The figure for A4 continuous is incorrect for March – the number sold should have been 1750
2 Add another column heading: TOTAL
                                   PER ITEM
3 Calculate the total sales for each item
4 Go to cell A1 and insert 2 rows – type an appropriate heading for the spreadsheet
5 Insert a further row after the column headings
6 Fill the above row with hyphens (–)
7 Using Global format command, format all cells containing figures to display currency with no decimal places
8 On completion, save as EX2.1 and print a copy of your spreadsheet.

Clear the screen prior to commencing Exercise 2.2.

Spreadsheet Exercise 2.2

Recall Exercises 2.1 and carry out the following tasks:

1 After March, insert a further 3 columns, using the same command as for adding rows
2 Enter the following headings and data:

APR	MAY	JUNE
1200	1000	900
1200	1250	1300
1050	1500	900
2523	2100	1850
1200	500	1500
2200	2000	1700
500	600	780
350	550	180

3 Edit the heading in A1 to read MONTHLY SALES
4 Edit the formulae in the TOTAL PER ITEM column to include the columns which you have just added
5 Copy the formula for March's total to the additional columns
6 Print out only the side headings, your 3 new columns and the appropriate totals
7 On completion, save your document as EX2.2

Spreadsheet Exercise 2.3

Recall Exercise 2.2, redisplaying all columns:

1 If your program has the facility, save as SS2.3 only the side and column headings
2 If your program does not have this facility, erase the range containing all figures, but not containing formulae, and save the worksheet as SS2.3
3 Take a printout of file SS2.3
4 Retrieve EX2.2 and take a printout of the entire spreadsheet
5 Clear the screen before proceeding to Exercise 3

Spreadsheet Exercise 3

The following exercise is a consolidation of some of the commands which you have used in Exercises 2 to 2.3:

1 Prepare a spreadsheet using the following information, increasing the width of column A as required.

EXPENSE ACCOUNT – January/March

EXPENSE	JAN	FEB	MAR	TOTAL
Petrol	56	70	59	
Entertainment	115	102	30	
Travel	70	25	15	
Sundry	45	31	20	
TOTAL				

2 Calculate the totals as indicated
3 Display all numerical entries as currency with 2 decimal places
4 Take a printout
5 Insert a row after Entertainment to incorporate the following:
   Child Minding   120   150   105
6 Copy formulae as required
7 Centre all headings over the columns
8 On completion, save as EX3 and print 2 copies of your spreadsheet – one displaying formulae as text

Spreadsheet Exercise 4

The following student records require to be entered into a spreadsheet:

Student's Name	History	Geography	Maths	English	French
Patterson, Kirsteen	78	68	72	55	53
Anderson, Stuart	70	52	66	70	82
Donaldson, Ann	89	78	67	56	45
Boswell, Anne	67	89	64	78	80
Boyd, Suzanne	70	90	89	78	92
Carswell, Brian	67	89	89	90	91
Davidson, David	78	89	67	55	67
Inglis, Iain	67	62	72	69	73
Fraser, Allison	78	67	89	67	68
George, Paul	90	92	86	85	82
Baxter, Peter	60	55	56	78	90
Graham, Kimberley	86	84	89	90	82
Hatherley, Simon	77	67	78	69	55
Adams, Neil	60	55	78	55	61
King, Andrew	78	72	69	66	59
Latimer, Thomas	89	85	82	79	76
Matthews, Jason	76	56	55	67	50
Mathieson, Martin	76	79	89	68	65
Johnstone, Gillian	89	82	79	69	72
Rae, Gillian	90	92	95	89	85

Number of students   20

1 Calculate the students' total marks by inserting the first formula and using the copy command thereafter.
2 Calculate the total marks per subject for all students as per step 1 above
3 Calculate the average class mark per subject using a mixture of relative and absolute cell referencing based on the cell containing the number of students
4 Calculate the average mark per student
5 Format all ranges containing averages to 0 decimal places
6 On completion, save your file as EX4, taking 2 printouts – one showing formulae as text

Spreadsheet Exercise 4.1

Retrieve Exercise 4 and make the following alterations:

1 Sort the data into alphabetical order
2 Move the column headed **French** to be displayed after **Geography**
3 Save this worksheet as Exercise 4.1, taking a further printout
4 Retrieve Exercise 4, repeating the above steps and saving it as EX4.2
5 Using the **File Combine** function, consolidate Exercises 4.1 and 4.2
6 Edit the cell containing the total number of students to read 20
7 Edit the Average Per Student formulae to give the same answers as Exercise 4
8 Edit the formula which produces the average to give the same answers as Exercise 4
9 Take a printout of this combined file
10 The marks allocated to Gillian Rae and Kirsteen Patterson are incorrect – erase the range containing these marks but not the names of the students
11 Take a further printout of this file

Spreadsheet Exercise 5

Prepare the following spreadsheet which will be used to calculate the employee wages of a small company:

NAME	WORKS NUMBER	HOURLY RATE	HOURS WORKED	GROSS	TAX	NET
Williamson H	240	7	40			
Baxter A	232	7.5	40			
Baxter C	256	6	35			
Crawford A	245	7.5	37			
Fraser C D	233	6.5	40	Wages.		
Henderson A	257	7	40			
Young A J	241	7.5	35			
Anderson J P	231	7.5	40			

1 Increase the width of column A as necessary
2 Using the **Format** command, format columns C, E, F and G to display currency
3 Calculate the weekly gross, inserting a formula to multiply the hourly rate by the hours worked
4 Deduct standard rate tax of 25% from the gross pay
5 Calculate the weekly net by subtracting the tax from the gross
6 On completion, save as EX5 and print your worksheet

Spreadsheet Exercise 5.1

A J Young should have received an increase of 50p per hour from the beginning of this week (Exercise 5).

1 Make the above amendment, taking a total of the amount of cash which is required to be withdrawn from the bank in order to prepare the wages
2 Sort the employees into alphabetical order
3 Save as EX5.1 and print 2 copies of your worksheet – one displaying formulae as text

Spreadsheet Exercise 5.2

The following overtime figures require to be included in the calculations.

Anderson, J P	(231)	4 hours at time + half
Baxter, A	(232)	4 hours at time + half, 2 hours at double time
Crawford, A	(245)	6 hours at time + half, 4 hours at double time
Henderson, A	(257)	5 hours at time + half, 2 hours at double time
Young, A J	(241)	5 hours at time + half, 4 hours at double time

1 Insert a further 3 columns before **GROSS**, using the following headings:

| O/T | O/T | O/T |
| X 1.5 | X 2 | PAY |

2 Set Calculation to manual
3 Calculate the overtime pay at the appropriate rate, formatting the columns to currency with 2 decimal places
4 Set Calculation to automatic
5 Edit the formulae as necessary
   (Edit Gross pay figures to include overtime pay)
6 Change heading HOURS WORKED to BASIC HOURS
7 Edit Tax and Net formulae as appropriate
8 Save as EX5.2 and print 2 copies of your worksheet – one displaying formulae as text

Spreadsheet Exercise 5.3

1 Retrieve EX5.2 and save the headings only as EX5.3
2 Retrieve EX5.3 (the file containing only the headings) and insert only the appropriate formulae into the relevant cells, copying them as required
3 Intake the range containing the hourly rate and basic hours from EX5.2
4 Print out one copy of the entire file

Spreadsheet Exercise 5.4

1 Retrieve EX5.2
2 Count the number of employees, using the appropriate formula
3 Find out the average weekly take-home pay
4 Find out the maximum and minimum weekly take-home pay
5 On completion, save your file as EX5.4, taking 2 printouts – one displaying formulae as text

Spreadsheet Exercise 6

1 Retrieve EX3 from your disk and prepare a bar chart showing how the different expenditures compare for each of the 3 months.

   1.1   The chart should be headed EXPENSE ACCOUNT
   1.2   You should use Legends to indicate each expense shading
   1.3   Upon completion, save and print a copy of your chart

2 Retrieve EX3 from your disk and prepare a pie chart for the item **Child Minding** in order to illustrate how the expense is distributed over the period.

   2.1   The chart should be headed up EXPENSE ACCOUNT on the first line and CHILD MINDING on the second line of the heading
   2.2   Use appropriate shadings for your chart
   2.3   Upon completion, save and print a copy of your chart

Spreadsheet Exercise 7

1 Retrieve EX4 from your disk and prepare a bar chart and a pie chart for the results of Ann Donaldson in order that these may be presented to her guidance teacher

   1.1   Use an appropriate heading on both charts
   1.2   Use shading where required
   1.3   Save and print copies of both charts

2 Retrieve the bar chart from the above section

   2.1   Change this chart to a stacked bar and add the results of Anne Boswell and Suzanne Boyd
   2.2   Amend the heading where necessary
   2.3   Save and print a copy of this chart

Expense 1

Spreadsheet Exercise 8

It is important that you should know how to use the back-up facility of the program which you are using, so that you have an additional copy of your files should anything happen to them.

   You will require to have an additional disk to carry out the following exercise properly. However, if this is not possible, you should simply back-up your files using the same disk.

1 Make back-up (security) copies of the following files:

   EX2.1   EX2.2   EX2.3

2 Should you require to allocate new file names, the following should be used:

   EXER2.1   EXER2.2   EXER2.3

3 Display your file directory in order to check that these back-up files are present.
4 Take a printout of your directory, using 'print screen' where necessary

Spreadsheet Exercise 9

Intake from your word processing program the table saved in Exercise 8.

1 Calculate the total sales per region and the total sales per month
2 Calculate the average sales per month and the average sales per region.
3 On completion, save the worksheet as EX9 and print one copy of your file.

Spreadsheet Exercise 9.1

Intake from your word processing program the table saved in Exercise 8.1.

1 Using an IF condition formula, add 10% to any seat sales currently selling for less than £400
2 Copy the entire contents of the file to row 40 (this will give you 2 copies of your spreadsheet in this file)
3 Display all formulae from row 40 as text
4 On completion, print out a copy of the entire file

Spreadsheet solutions

Spreadsheet Exercise 1

CHEQUE BOOK ACCOUNT – JANUARY

CHEQUE	DATE	DESCRPT	CHEQUE AMOUNT	DEPOSIT AMOUNT	BALANCE
	Jan 03				1250
	Jan 08	Groceries	90		
	Jan 10	Petrol	30		
	Jan 12	Butcher	15		
	Jan 13	Material	45		
	Jan 13	Comm Chrg	65		
	Jan 15	Groceries	45		
	Jan 17	Butcher	12		
	Jan 20	Elect	110		
	Jan 20	Petrol	25		
	Jan 21	Gas	80		
	Jan 22	Groceries	25		
	Jan 23	Credit	96		
	Jan 25	B. Soc	360		
	Jan 26	Insurance	56		
	Jan 28	Car Insur	210		
	Jan 30	Salary		1015	

Spreadsheet Exercise 1.1

CHEQUE BOOK ACCOUNT – JANUARY

CHEQUE	DATE	DESCRPT	CHEQUE AMOUNT	DEPOSIT AMOUNT	BALANCE
	Jan 03				1250
10607	Jan 08	Groceries	90		
10608	Jan 10	Petrol	30		
10609	Jan 12	Butcher	15		
10610	Jan 13	Material	45		
10611	Jan 13	Comm Chrg	65		
10612	Jan 15	Groceries	45		
10613	Jan 17	Butcher	12		
10614	Jan 20	Elect	110		
10615	Jan 20	Petrol	25		
10616	Jan 21	Gas	80		
10617	Jan 22	Groceries	25		
10618	Jan 23	Credit	96		
10619	Jan 25	B. Soc	360		
10620	Jan 26	Insurance	56		
10621	Jan 28	Car Insur	210		
			@SUM(D6..D20)		+F5−D21
	Jan 30	Salary		1015	+F21+E22

CHEQUE BOOK ACCOUNT — JANUARY

CHEQUE	DATE	DESCRPT	CHEQUE AMOUNT	DEPOSIT AMOUNT	BALANCE
	Jan 03				********
10607	Jan 08	Groceries	₤90.00		
10608	Jan 10	Petrol	₤30.00		
10609	Jan 12	Butcher	₤15.00		
10610	Jan 13	Material	₤45.00		
10611	Jan 13	Comm Chrg	₤65.00		
10612	Jan 15	Groceries	₤45.00		
10613	Jan 17	Butcher	₤12.00		
10614	Jan 20	Elect	₤110.00		
10615	Jan 20	Petrol	₤25.00		
10616	Jan 21	Gas	₤80.00		
10617	Jan 22	Groceries	₤25.00		
10618	Jan 23	Credit	₤96.00		
10619	Jan 25	B. Soc	₤360.00		
10620	Jan 26	Insurance	₤56.00		
10621	Jan 28	Car Insur	₤210.00		
			₤1,264.00		(₤14.00)
	Jan 30	Salary			******************

Spreadsheet Exercise 1.2

CHEQUE BOOK ACCOUNT — JANUARY

CHEQUE	DATE	DESCRPT	CHEQUE AMOUNT	DEPOSIT AMOUNT	BALANCE
	Jan 03				₤1,250
10607	Jan 08	Groceries	₤90.00		
10608	Jan 10	Petrol	₤30.00		
10609	Jan 12	Butcher	₤15.00		
10610	Jan 13	Material	₤45.00		
10611	Jan 13	Comm Charge	₤65.00		
10612	Jan 15	Groceries	₤45.00		
10613	Jan 17	Butcher	₤12.00		
10614	Jan 20	Electricity	₤110.00		
10615	Jan 20	Petrol	₤25.00		
10616	Jan 21	Gas	₤80.00		
10617	Jan 22	Groceries	₤25.00		
10618	Jan 23	Credit	₤96.00		
10619	Jan 25	B. Soc	₤360.00		
10620	Jan 26	Insurance	₤56.00		
10621	Jan 28	Car Insur	₤210.00		
			₤1,264.00		(₤14.00)
	Jan 30	Salary		₤1,015	₤1,001.00

Spreadsheet Exercise 2

PRODUCT	JAN	FEB	MAR
5 1/4" DISKS	1500	1200	1300
3 1/2" DISKS	1200	1350	1500
A4 FORM FEED	1050	1200	900
A4 CONTINUOUS	2000	2100	1950
A3 FORM FEED	900	700	1200
A3 CONTINUOUS	2500	2100	1900
CARBON RIBBONS	750	650	780
FABRIC RIBBONS	250	450	170
	10150	9750	9700

Spreadsheet Exercise 2 (formulae as text)

PRODUCT	JAN	FEB	MAR
5 1/4" DISKS	1500	1200	1300
3 1/2" DISKS	1200	1350	1500
A4 FORM FEED	1050	1200	900
A4 CONTINUOUS	2000	2100	1950
A3 FORM FEED	900	700	1200
A3 CONTINUOUS	2500	2100	1900
CARBON RIBBONS	750	650	780
FABRIC RIBBONS	250	450	170
	@SUM(B3..B10)	@SUM(C3..C10)	@SUM(D3..D10)

Spreadsheet Exercise 2.1

SALES FIGURES – JANUARY/MARCH

PRODUCT	JAN	FEB	MAR	TOTAL PER ITEM
5 1/4" DISKS	£1,500	£1,200	£1,300	£4,000
3 1/2" DISKS	£1,200	£1,350	£1,500	£4,050
A4 FORM FEED	£1,050	£1,200	£900	£3,150
A4 CONTINUOUS	£2,000	£2,100	£1,750	£5,850
A3 FORM FEED	£900	£700	£1,200	£2,800
A3 CONTINUOUS	£2,500	£2,100	£1,900	£6,500
CARBON RIBBONS	£750	£650	£780	£2,180
FABRIC RIBBONS	£250	£450	£170	£870
	£10,150	£9,750	£9,500	£29,400

Spreadsheet Exercise 2.2

PRODUCT	APR	MAY	JUNE	TOTAL PER ITEM
5 1/4" DISKS	£1,200	£1,000	£900	£7,100
3 1/2" DISKS	£1,200	£1,250	£1,300	£7,800
A4 FORM FEED	£1,050	£1,500	£900	£6,600
A4 CONTINUOUS	£2,523	£2,100	£1,850	£12,323
A3 FORM FEED	£1,200	£500	£1,500	£6,000
A3 CONTINUOUS	£2,200	£2,000	£1,700	£12,400
CARBON RIBBONS	£500	£600	£780	£4,060
FABRIC RIBBONS	£350	£550	£180	£1,950
	£10,223	£9,500	£9,110	£58,233

Spreadsheet Exercise 2.3

PRODUCT	JAN	FEB	MAR	APR	MAY	JUNE	TOTAL PER ITEM
5 1/4" DISKS							£0
3 1/2" DISKS							£0
A4 FORM FEED							£0
A4 CONTINUOUS							£0
A3 FORM FEED							£0
A3 CONTINUOUS							£0
CARBON RIBBONS							£0
FABRIC RIBBONS							£0
	£0	£0	£0	£0	£0	£0	£0

PRODUCT	JAN	FEB	MAR	APR	MAY	JUNE	TOTAL PER ITEM
5 1/4" DISKS	£1,500	£1,200	£1,300	£1,200	£1,000	£900	£7,100
3 1/2" DISKS	£1,200	£1,350	£1,500	£1,200	£1,250	£1,300	£7,800
A4 FORM FEED	£1,050	£1,200	£900	£1,050	£1,500	£900	£6,600
A4 CONTINUOUS	£2,000	£2,100	£1,750	£2,523	£2,100	£1,850	£12,323
A3 FORM FEED	£900	£700	£1,200	£1,200	£500	£1,500	£6,000
A3 CONTINUOUS	£2,500	£2,100	£1,900	£2,200	£2,000	£1,700	£12,400
CARBON RIBBONS	£750	£650	£780	£500	£600	£780	£4,060
FABRIC RIBBONS	£250	£450	£170	£350	£550	£180	£1,950
	£10,150	£9,750	£9,500	£10,223	£9,500	£9,110	£58,233

Spreadsheet Exercise 3

EXPENSE ACCOUNT — January/March

EXPENSE	JAN	FEB	MAR	TOTAL
Petrol	£56.00	£70.00	£59.00	£185.00
Entertainment	£115.00	£102.00	£30.00	£247.00
Travel	£70.00	£25.00	£15.00	£110.00
Sundry	£45.00	£31.00	£20.00	£96.00
TOTAL	£286.00	£228.00	£124.00	£638.00

EXPENSE ACCOUNT — January/March

EXPENSE	JAN	FEB	MAR	TOTAL
Petrol	£56.00	£70.00	£59.00	£185.00
Entertainment	£115.00	£102.00	£30.00	£247.00
Child Minding	£120.00	£150.00	£105.00	£375.00
Travel	£70.00	£25.00	£15.00	£110.00
Sundry	£45.00	£31.00	£20.00	£96.00
TOTAL	£406.00	£378.00	£229.00	£1,013.00

EXPENSE ACCOUNT — January/March

EXPENSE	JAN	FEB	MAR	TOTAL
Petrol	£56.00	£70.00	£59.00	@SUM(B5..D5)
Entertainment	£115.00	£102.00	£30.00	@SUM(B7..D7)
Child Minding	£120.00	£150.00	£105.00	@SUM(B9..D9)
Travel	£70.00	£25.00	£15.00	@SUM(B11..D11)
Sundry	£45.00	£31.00	£20.00	@SUM(B13..D13)
TOTAL	@SUM(B5..B13)	@SUM(C5..C13)	@SUM(D5..D13)	@SUM(E5..E13)

Spreadsheet Exercise 4

STUDENT'S NAME	HISTORY	GEOGRAPHY	MATHS	ENGLISH	FRENCH	TOTAL PER STUDENT	AVERAGE PER STUDENT
Patterson, Kirsteen	78	68	72	55	53	326	65
Anderson, Stuart	70	52	66	70	82	340	68
Donaldson, Ann	89	78	67	56	45	335	67
Boswell, Anne	67	89	64	78	80	378	76
Boyd, Suzanne	70	90	89	78	92	419	84
Carswell, Brian	67	89	89	90	91	426	85
Davidson, David	78	89	67	55	67	356	71
Inglis, Iain	67	62	72	69	73	343	69
Fraser. Allison	78	67	89	67	68	369	74
George, Paul	90	92	86	85	82	435	87
Baxter, Peter	60	55	56	78	90	339	68
Graham, Kimberley	86	84	89	90	82	431	86
Hatherley, Simon	77	67	78	69	55	346	69
Adams, Neil	60	55	78	55	61	309	62
King, Andrew	78	72	69	66	59	344	69
Latimer, Thomas	89	85	82	79	76	411	82
Matthews, Jason	76	56	55	67	50	304	61
Mathieson, Martin	76	79	89	68	65	377	75
Johnstone, Gillian	89	82	79	69	72	391	78
Rae, Gillian	90	92	95	89	85	451	90
TOTALS	1535	1503	1531	1433	1428	AVERAGE	
	77	75	77	72	71	CLASS MARK=	74
Number of Students	20						

STUDENT'S NAME	HISTORY	GEOGRAPHY	MATHS	ENGLISH	FRENCH	TOTAL PER STUDENT	AVERAGE PER STUDENT
Patterson, Kirsteen	78	68	72	55	53	@SUM(B3..F3)	+G3/5
Anderson, Stuart	70	52	66	70	82	@SUM(B4..F4)	+G4/5
Donaldson, Ann	89	78	67	56	45	@SUM(B5..F5)	+G5/5
Boswell, Anne	67	89	64	78	80	@SUM(B6..F6)	+G6/5
Boyd, Suzanne	70	90	89	78	92	@SUM(B7..F7)	+G7/5
Carswell, Brian	67	89	89	90	91	@SUM(B8..F8)	+G8/5
Davidson, David	78	89	67	55	67	@SUM(B9..F9)	+G9/5
Inglis, Iain	67	62	72	69	73	@SUM(B10..F10)	+G10/5
Fraser. Allison	78	67	89	67	68	@SUM(B11..F11)	+G11/5
George, Paul	90	92	86	85	82	@SUM(B12..F12)	+G12/5
Baxter, Peter	60	55	56	78	90	@SUM(B13..F13)	+G13/5
Graham, Kimberley	86	84	89	90	82	@SUM(B14..F14)	+G14/5
Hatherley, Simon	77	67	78	69	55	@SUM(B15..F15)	+G15/5
Adams, Neil	60	55	78	55	61	@SUM(B16..F16)	+G16/5
King, Andrew	78	72	69	66	59	@SUM(B17..F17)	+G17/5
Latimer, Thomas	89	85	82	79	76	@SUM(B18..F18)	+G18/5
Matthews, Jason	76	56	55	67	50	@SUM(B19..F19)	+G19/5
Mathieson, Martin	76	79	89	68	65	@SUM(B20..F20)	+G20/5
Johnstone, Gillian	89	82	79	69	72	@SUM(B21..F21)	+G21/5
Rae, Gillian	90	92	95	89	85	@SUM(B22..F22)	+G22/5
TOTALS	@SUM(B3..B22)	@SUM(C3..C22)	@SUM(D3..D22)	@SUM(E3..E22)	@SUM(F3..F22)	AVERAGE	
	+B24/$B$27	+C24/$B$27	+D24/$B$27	+E24/$B$27	+F24/$B$27	CLASS MARK= @SUM(H3..H22)/$B$27	
Number of Students	20						

Spreadsheet Exercise 4 (alternative formula for calculating average)

STUDENT'S NAME	HISTORY	GEOGRAPHY	MATHS	ENGLISH	FRENCH	TOTAL PER STUDENT	AVERAGE PER STUDENT
Patterson, Kirsteen	78	68	72	55	53	326	@AVG(B3..F3)
Anderson, Stuart	70	52	66	70	82	340	@AVG(B4..F4)
Donaldson, Ann	89	78	67	56	45	335	@AVG(B5..F5)
Boswell, Anne	67	89	64	78	80	378	@AVG(B6..F6)
Boyd, Suzanne	70	90	89	78	92	419	@AVG(B7..F7)
Carswell, Brian	67	89	89	90	91	426	@AVG(B8..F8)
Davidson, David	78	89	67	55	67	356	@AVG(B9..F9)
Inglis, Iain	67	62	72	69	73	343	@AVG(B10..F10)
Fraser. Allison	78	67	89	67	68	369	@AVG(B11..F11)
George, Paul	90	92	86	85	82	435	@AVG(B12..F12)
Baxter, Peter	60	55	56	78	90	339	@AVG(B13..F13)
Graham, Kimberley	86	84	89	90	82	431	@AVG(B14..F14)
Hatherley, Simon	77	67	78	69	55	346	@AVG(B15..F15)
Adams, Neil	60	55	78	55	61	309	@AVG(B16..F16)
King, Andrew	78	72	69	66	59	344	@AVG(B17..F17)
Latimer, Thomas	89	85	82	79	76	411	@AVG(B18..F18)
Matthews, Jason	76	56	55	67	50	304	@AVG(B19..F19)
Mathieson, Martin	76	79	89	68	65	377	@AVG(B20..F20)
Johnstone, Gillian	89	82	79	69	72	391	@AVG(B21..F21)
Rae, Gillian	90	92	95	89	85	451	@AVG(B22..F22)
TOTALS	1535	1503	1531	1433	1428	AVERAGE	
	76.75	75.15	76.55	71.65	71.4	CLASS MARK=	@AVG(B25..F25)
Number of Students	20						

Spreadsheet Exercise 4.1 (1)

STUDENT'S NAME	HISTORY	GEOGRAPHY	FRENCH	MATHS	ENGLISH	TOTAL PER STUDENT	AVERAGE PER STUDENT
Adams, Neil	60	55	61	78	55	309	62
Anderson, Stuart	70	52	82	66	70	340	68
Baxter, Peter	60	55	90	56	78	339	68
Boswell, Anne	67	89	80	64	78	378	76
Boyd, Suzanne	70	90	92	89	78	419	84
Carswell, Brian	67	89	91	89	90	426	85
Davidson, David	78	89	67	67	55	356	71
Donaldson, Ann	89	78	45	67	56	335	67
Fraser. Allison	78	67	68	89	67	369	74
George, Paul	90	92	82	86	85	435	87
Graham, Kimberley	86	84	82	89	90	431	86
Hatherley, Simon	77	67	55	78	69	346	69
Inglis, Iain	67	62	73	72	69	343	69
Johnstone, Gillian	89	82	72	79	69	391	78
King, Andrew	78	72	59	69	66	344	69
Latimer, Thomas	89	85	76	82	79	411	82
Mathieson, Martin	76	79	65	89	68	377	75
Matthews, Jason	76	56	50	55	67	304	61
Patterson, Kirsteen	78	68	53	72	55	326	65
Rae, Gillian	90	92	85	95	89	451	90
TOTALS	1535	1503	1428	1531	1433	AVERAGE	
	77	75	71	77	72	CLASS MARK=	74

Number of Students	20

Spreadsheet Exercise 4.1 (2)

STUDENT'S NAME	HISTORY	GEOGRAPHY	FRENCH	MATHS	ENGLISH	TOTAL PER STUDENT	AVERAGE PER STUDENT
Adams, Neil	120	110	122	156	110	618	62
Anderson, Stuart	140	104	164	132	140	680	68
Baxter, Peter	120	110	180	112	156	678	68
Boswell, Anne	134	178	160	128	156	756	76
Boyd, Suzanne	140	180	184	178	156	838	84
Carswell, Brian	134	178	182	178	180	852	85
Davidson, David	156	178	134	134	110	712	71
Donaldson, Ann	178	156	90	134	112	670	67
Fraser. Allison	156	134	136	178	134	738	74
George, Paul	180	184	164	172	170	870	87
Graham, Kimberley	172	168	164	178	180	862	86
Hatherley, Simon	154	134	110	156	138	692	69
Inglis, Iain	134	124	146	144	138	686	69
Johnstone, Gillian	178	164	144	158	138	782	78
King, Andrew	156	144	118	138	132	688	69
Latimer, Thomas	178	170	152	164	158	822	82
Mathieson, Martin	152	158	130	178	136	754	75
Matthews, Jason	152	112	100	110	134	608	61
Patterson, Kirsteen	156	136	106	144	110	652	65
Rae, Gillian	180	184	170	190	178	902	90
TOTALS	3070	3006	2856	3062	2866	AVERAGE	
	77	75	71	77	72	CLASS MARK=	74

Number of Students	20

Spreadsheet Exercise 4.1 (3)

STUDENT'S NAME	HISTORY	GEOGRAPHY	FRENCH	MATHS	ENGLISH	TOTAL PER STUDENT	AVERAGE PER STUDENT
Adams, Neil	120	110	122	156	110	618	62
Anderson, Stuart	140	104	164	132	140	680	68
Baxter, Peter	120	110	180	112	156	678	68
Boswell, Anne	134	178	160	128	156	756	76
Boyd, Suzanne	140	180	184	178	156	838	84
Carswell, Brian	134	178	182	178	180	852	85
Davidson, David	156	178	134	134	110	712	71
Donaldson, Ann	178	156	90	134	112	670	67
Fraser. Allison	156	134	136	178	134	738	74
George, Paul	180	184	164	172	170	870	87
Graham, Kimberley	172	168	164	178	180	862	86
Hatherley, Simon	154	134	110	156	138	692	69
Inglis, Iain	134	124	146	144	138	686	69
Johnstone, Gillian	178	164	144	158	138	782	78
King, Andrew	156	144	118	138	132	688	69
Latimer, Thomas	178	170	152	164	158	822	82
Mathieson, Martin	152	158	130	178	136	754	75
Matthews, Jason	152	112	100	110	134	608	61
Patterson, Kirsteen						0	0
Rae, Gillian						0	0
TOTALS	2734	2686	2580	2728	2578	AVERAGE	
	68	67	65	68	64	CLASS MARK=	67

Number of Students   20

Spreadsheet Exercise 5

NAME	WORKS NUMBER	HOURLY RATE	HOURS WORKED	GROSS	TAX	NET
Williamson H	240	£7.00	40	£280.00	£70.00	£210.00
Baxter A	232	£7.50	40	£300.00	£75.00	£225.00
Baxter C	256	£6.00	35	£210.00	£52.50	£157.50
Crawford A	245	£7.50	37	£277.50	£69.38	£208.13
Fraser C D	233	£6.50	40	£260.00	£65.00	£195.00
Henderson A	257	£7.00	40	£280.00	£70.00	£210.00
Young A J	241	£7.50	35	£262.50	£65.63	£196.88
Anderson J P	231	£7.50	40	£300.00	£75.00	£225.00

Spreadsheet Exercise 5.1

NAME	WORKS NUMBER	HOURLY RATE	HOURS WORKED	GROSS	TAX	NET
Anderson J P	231	£7.50	40	£300.00	£75.00	£225.00
Baxter A	232	£7.50	40	£300.00	£75.00	£225.00
Baxter C	256	£6.00	35	£210.00	£52.50	£157.50
Crawford A	245	£7.50	37	£277.50	£69.38	£208.13
Fraser C D	233	£6.50	40	£260.00	£65.00	£195.00
Henderson A	257	£7.00	40	£280.00	£70.00	£210.00
Williamson H	240	£7.00	40	£280.00	£70.00	£210.00
Young A J	241	£8.00	35	£280.00	£70.00	£210.00
						£1,640.63

NAME	WORKS NUMBER	HOURLY RATE	HOURS WORKED	GROSS	TAX	NET
Anderson J P	231	£7.50	40	+C4*D4	+E4*0.25	+E4-F4
Baxter A	232	£7.50	40	+C5*D5	+E5*0.25	+E5-F5
Baxter C	256	£6.00	35	+C6*D6	+E6*0.25	+E6-F6
Crawford A	245	£7.50	37	+C7*D7	+E7*0.25	+E7-F7
Fraser C D	233	£6.50	40	+C8*D8	+E8*0.25	+E8-F8
Henderson A	257	£7.00	40	+C9*D9	+E9*0.25	+E9-F9
Williamson H	240	£7.00	40	+C10*D10	+E10*0.25	+E10-F10
Young A J	241	£8.00	35	+C11*D11	+E11*0.25	+E11-F11
						@SUM(G4..G11)

Spreadsheet Exercise 5.2

NAME	WORKS NUMBER	HOURLY RATE	BASIC HOURS	O/T X 1.5	O/T X 2	O/T PAY	GROSS	TAX	NET
Anderson JP	231	£7.50	40	4		£45.00	£345.00	£86.25	£258.75
Baxter A	232	£7.50	40	4	2	£75.00	£375.00	£93.75	£281.25
Baxter C	256	£6.00	35			£0.00	£210.00	£52.50	£157.50
Crawford A	245	£7.50	37	6	4	£127.50	£405.00	£101.25	£303.75
Fraser C D	233	£6.50	40			£0.00	£260.00	£65.00	£195.00
Henderson A	257	£7.00	40	5	2	£80.50	£360.50	£90.13	£270.38
Williamson H	240	£7.00	40			£0.00	£280.00	£70.00	£210.00
Young A J	241	£8.00	35	5	4	£124.00	£404.00	£101.00	£303.00

£1,979.63

NAME	WORKS NUMBER	HOURLY RATE	BASIC HOURS	O/T X 1.5	O/T X 2	O/T PAY	GROSS	TAX	NET
Anderson J P	231	£7.50	40	4		(C4*E4*1.5)(+C4*F4*2)	+C4*D4+G4	+H4*0.25	+H4-I4
Baxter A	232	£7.50	40	4	2	(+C5*E5*1.5)(+C5*F5*2)	+C5*D5+G5	+H5*0.25	+H5-I5
Baxter C	256	£6.00	35			(C6*E6*1.5)(+C6*F6*2)	+C6*D6+G6	+H6*0.25	+H6-I6
Crawford A	245	£7.50	37	6	4	(C7*E7*1.5)(+C7*F7*2)	+C7*D7+G7	+H7*0.25	+H7-I7
Fraser CD	233	£6.50	40			(C8*E8*1.5)(+C8*F8*2)	+C8*D8+G8	+H8*0.25	+H8-18
Henderson A	257	£7.00	40	5	2	(C9*E9*1.5)(+C9*F9*2)	+C9*D9+G9	+H9*0.25	+H9-I9
Williamson H	240	£7.00	40			(C10*E10*1.5)(+C10*F10*2)	+C10*D10+	+H10*0.2	+H10-I10
Young A J	241	£8.00	35	5	4	(C11*E11*1/5)(+C11*F11*2)	+C11*D11+	+H11*0.2	+H11-I11

@SUM(J4..J11)

Spreadsheet Exercise 5.3

NAME	WORKS NUMBER	HOURLY RATE	BASIC HOURS	O/T X 1.5	O/T X 2	O/T PAY	GROSS	TAX	NET
Anderson J P						£0.00	£0.00	£0.00	£0.00
Baxter A						£0.00	£0.00	£0.00	£0.00
Baxter C						£0.00	£0.00	£0.00	£0.00
Crawford A						£0.00	£0.00	£0.00	£0.00
Fraser C D						£0.00	£0.00	£0.00	£0.00
Henderson A						£0.00	£0.00	£0.00	£0.00
Williamson H						£0.00	£0.00	£0.00	£0.00
Young A J						£0.00	£0.00	£0.00	£0.00
									£0.00

NAME	WORKS NUMBER	HOURLY RATE	BASIC HOURS	O/T X 1.5	O/T X 2	O/T PAY	GROSS	TAX	NET
Anderson J P		£7.50	40			£0.00	£300.00	£75.00	£225.00
Baxter A		£7.50	40			£0.00	£300.00	£75.00	£225.00
Baxter C		£6.00	35			£0.00	£210.00	£52.50	£157.50
Crawford A		£7.50	37			£0.00	£277.50	£69.38	£208.13
Fraser C D		£6.50	40			£0.00	£260.00	£65.00	£195.00
Henderson A		£7.00	40			£0.00	£280.00	£70.00	£210.00
Williamson H		£7.00	40			£0.00	£280.00	£70.00	£210.00
Young A J		£8.00	35			£0.00	£280.00	£70.00	£210.00
									£1,640.63

Spreadsheet Exercise 5.4 (1)

NAME	WORKS NUMBER	HOURLY RATE	BASIC HOURS	O/T X 1.5	O/T X 2	O/T PAY	GROSS	TAX	NET
Anderson J P	231	7.50	40	4		45.00	345.00	86.25	258.75
Baxter A	232	7.50	40	4	2	75.00	375.00	93.75	281.25
Baxter C	256	6.00	35			0.00	210.00	52.50	157.50
Crawford A	245	7.50	37	6	4	127.50	405.00	101.25	303.75
Fraser C D	233	6.50	40			0.00	260.00	65.00	195.00
Henderson A	257	7.00	40	5	2	80.50	360.50	90.13	270.38
Williamson H	240	7.00	40			0.00	280.00	70.00	210.00
Young A J	241	8.00	35	5	4	124.00	404.00	101.00	303.00

1979.63

No of Employees   8

Average Weekly
Take-home Pay   247.45

Maximum Weekly
Take-home Pay   303.75

Minimum Weekly
Take-home Pay   157.50

Spreadsheet Exercise 5.4 (2)

NAME	WORKS NUMBER	HOURLY RATE	BASIC HOURS	O/T X 1.5	O/T X 2	O/T PAY	GROSS	TAX	NET
Anderson J P	231	7.50	40	4		45.00	345.00	86.25	258.75
Baxter A	232	7.50	40	4	2	75.00	375.00	93.75	281.25
Baxter C	256	6.00	35			0.00	210.00	52.50	157.50
Crawford A	245	7.50	37	6	4	127.50	405.00	101.25	303.75
Fraser C D	233	6.50	40			0.00	260.00	65.00	195.00
Henderson A	257	7.00	40	5	2	80.50	360.50	90.13	270.38
Williamson H	240	7.00	40			0.00	280.00	70.00	210.00
Young A J	241	8.00	35	5	4	124.00	404.00	101.00	303.00

1979.63

No of Employees   COUNT(A7..A14)

Average Weekly
Take-home Pay   AVG(J7..J14)

Maximum Weekly
Take-home Pay   MAX(J7..J14)

Minimum Weekly
Take-home Pay   MIN(J7..J14)

Spreadsheet Exercise 6 (1)

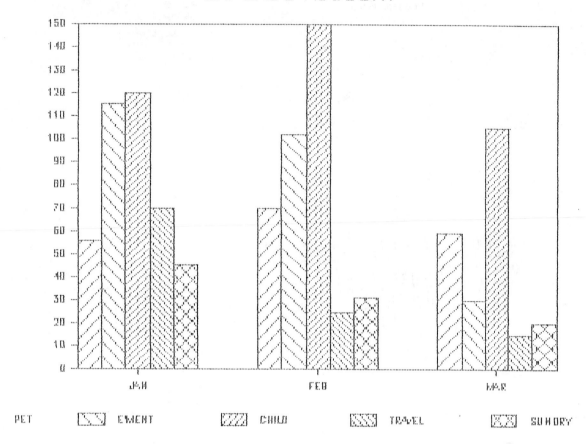

Spreadsheet Exercise 6 (2)

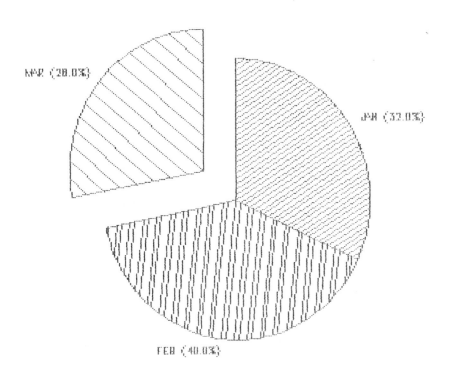

EXPENSE ACCOUNT

CHILD MINDING

MAR (28.0%)

JAN (32.0%)

FEB (40.0%)

Spreadsheet Exercise 7 (1) — bar chart

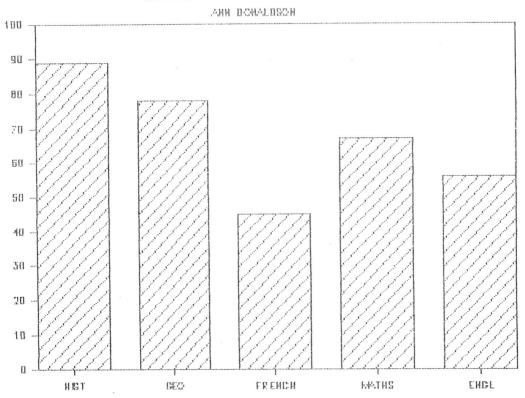

EXAMINATION RESULTS

ANN DONALDSON

HIST GEO FRENCH MATHS ENGL

Spreadsheet Exercise 7 (1) – pie chart

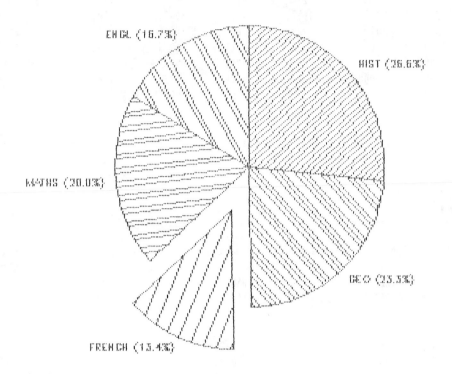

EXAMINATION RESULTS

ANN DONALDSON

ENGL (16.7%)

HIST (26.63%)

MATHS (30.03%)

GEO (35.53%)

FRENCH (15.43%)

Spreadsheet Exercise 7 (2)

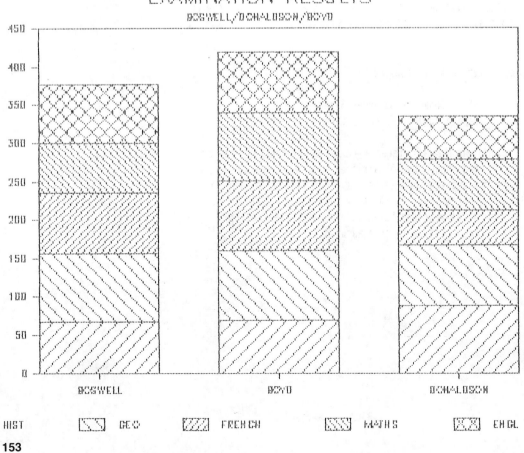

EXAMINATION RESULTS

BOSWELL/DONALDSON/BOYD

HIST ☐ GEO ☐ FRENCH ☐ MATHS ☐ ENGL

Spreadsheet Exercise 9

SALES FIGURES - JANUARY - JUNE

MONTH	CENTRAL	STRATHCYLDE	HIGHLAND	FIFE	BORDERS	MONTHLY TOTALS	MONTHLY AVERAGES
Jan	1230	1500	1520	1234	1120	6604	1321
Feb	1330	1231	1657	1657	1100	6975	1395
March	1230	1511	1200	1200	1600	6741	1348
April	1600	1100	1530	1530	1211	6971	1394
May	1177	1120	1000	1000	1341	5638	1128
June	1321	1345	900	1200	1211	5977	1195
	7888	7807	7807	7821	7583	38906	

AVERAGE MONTHLY							
SALES:	1315	1301	1301	1304	1264	6484	

Spreadsheet Exercise 9.1

SEAT SALES FARES (for travel until 13 March, travel completed by 20 March)

TO	FROM LONDON	NEW PRICE	GLASGOW	NEW PRICE	MANCHESTER	NEW PRICE
St Johns	419.95	419.95	-	0.00	-	0.00
Halifax	500.00	500.00	545.45	545.45	-	0.00
Gander	500.00	500.00	545.45	545.45	-	0.00
Montreal	319.45	351.40	399.50	439.45	-	0.00
Ottawa	319.00	350.90	399.50	439.45	-	0.00
Toronto	319.00	350.90	399.50	439.45	-	0.00
Winnipeg	379.00	416.90	-	0.00	-	0.00
Calgary	429.00	429.00	429.00	429.00	429.00	429.00
Edmonton	429.00	429.00	-	0.00	429.00	429.00
Vancouver	449.50	449.50	449.50	449.50	449.50	449.50

Weekend Supplement: £20 each way applied as follows:

UK to Canada - Saturday/Sunday
Canada to UK - Friday/Saturday

PLEASE NOTE: Transatlantic fares are subject to constant review
and change by the airlines. If you wish to
guarantee your fares, this can be done by making
full payment at the time of booking. Subject to
no alterations being made to your reservation -
your costing is then assured.

Spreadsheet Exercise 9.1 (formulae as text)

SEAT SALES FARES (for travel until 13 March, travel completed by 20 March)

TO	FROM LONDON		NEW PRICE	GLASGOW	NEW PRICE	MANCHESTER	NEW PRICE
St Johns	419.95	IF(B45<400,(+B45*0.1)+B45,+B45)		-	0.00	-	0.00
Halifax	500.00	IF(B46<400,(+B46*0.1)+B46,+B46)		545.45	545.45	-	0.00
Gander	500.00	IF(B47<400,(+B47*0.1)+B47,+B47)		545.45	545.45	-	0.00
Montreal	319.45	IF(B48<400,(+B48*0.1)+B48,+B48)		399.50	439.45	-	0.00
Ottawa	319.00	IF(B49<400,(+B49*0.1)+B49,+B49)		399.50	439.45	-	0.00
Toronto	319.00	IF(B50<400,(+B50*0.1)+B50,+B50)		399.50	439.45	-	0.00
Winnipeg	379.00	IF(B51<400,(+B51*0.1)+B51,+B51)		-	0.00	-	0.00
Calgary	429.00	IF(B52<400,(+B52*0.1)+B52,+B52)		429.00	429.00	429.00	429.00
Edmonton	429.00	IF(B53<400,(+B53*0.1)+B53,+B53)		-	0.00	429.00	429.00
Vancouver	449.50	IF(B54<400,(+B54*0.1)+B54,+B54)		449.50	449.50	449.50	449.50

Weekend Supplement: £20 each way applied as follows:

                                                 UK to Canada - Saturday/Sunday
                                                 Canada to UK - Friday/Saturday

PLEASE NOTE: Transatlantic fares are subject to
                                                 constant review and change by the
                                                 airlines. If you wish to guarantee
                                                 your fares, this can be done by making
                                                 full payment at the time of booking.
                                                 Subject to no alterations being made
                                                 to your reservation - your costing is
                                                 then assured.

Database exercises

What is a Database program?

A database program may be described very simply as an electronic filing system. The database file is set up according to the information which it will contain and the way in which it will be used. Thereafter, it can be used in a variety of ways to retrieve, sort, update and search for specific information.

A database program will search through files very quickly – far quicker than someone searching manually. The type of information which you could put into a database program would be the contents of the telephone directory. If you can imagine how long it would take you to locate everyone with a Glasgow telephone number from the telephone directory, this will give you an appreciation of how useful a computerised system of information retrieval can be. With a single command, the computer can locate and print the relevant information in seconds.

Database contents may also be used to merge print letters – some databases even have the facility to store the letter/label formats – so that a more personalised approach to mailing list printing may be achieved.

The more sophisticated (and normally more expensive) the database program is, the more versatile it will be.

Examples of Database Software:

DBase · Delta · DataEase

Summary

A database is a computer application progam which is used to store large volumes of information, thereafter searching and amending records as required.

Summary of new commands used in each exercise

The following is a summary of the commands you will need to know prior to commencing each exercise. Please check with your tutor or consult your manual for advice where necessary:

Exercise 1   Creating a database · Entering records · Printing from the database · Printing the database structure

Exercise 2   Consolidation of Exercise 1

Exercise 2.1   Amending the database structure

Exercise 3   Searching the database · Printing selected fields

Exercise 3.1   Amending the database structure · Editing records

Exercise 3.2   Searching on more than one field · Totalling a field · Editing records

Exercise 3.3   Deleting, adding and editing records · Searching on more than one field · Sorting and indexing the database · Using another database · Closing the index

Database Exercise 1

1 Create a database incorporating the following fields:

Field Name	Field Type	Field Length
COMPANY	Character	
ADDRESS1	Character	Decide on the field lengths required
TOWN	Character	
POSTCODE	Character	

2 Key the following information into the database file, remembering that database entries for people's names are normally entered surname first (eg Saunder J C Co Ltd) in order to facilitate sorting:

J C Saunder Co Ltd
21 High Street
EDINBURGH
EH2 5HH

Andrews Bros
55 North Byers Road
ABERDEEN
AB6 4PT

A & P Burrows
23 Anderston Drive
ABERDEEN
AB6 7BZ

Curtain Call
23 Coronation Street
EDINBURGH
EH2 7HB

Alderton & Simms Ltd
33 Ashton Road
EDINBURGH
EH5 5QQ

Jones & Dean PLC
33 Ice Drive
EDINBURGH
EH3 2NJ

Thomson & Co
57 High Street
ABERDEEN
AB1 1JT

Peebles Fashions Ltd
33 Mottles Green
LONDON
NW4

3 Upon completion, save and print a copy of your database contents

4 Print a copy of your database structure

Database Exercise 2

1 Create a database incorporating the following fields:

Field Name   Field Type   Field Length

NAME   Character
POSITION   Character
START DATE   Date   (Decide on the field lengths required)
PAY   Numerical

2 Key in the following data, remembering to enter the names commencing with the surname, eg Andrews, Alex:

Name	Position	Start Date	Pay
Alex Andrews	Supervisor	03.09.70	£16,252
James Smith	Assistant Manager	15.10.75	£18,000
Pauline Sneddon	Secretary	22.03.72	£13,500
Andrew Smith	Clerk	22.04.68	£10,025
Alison Drummond	Clerk	17.04.85	£6,900
Vivien McLean	Wages Clerk	21.01.88	£7,200
David Duncan	Manager	20.07.69	£20,000

3 Upon completion, save and print a copy of your database contents

4 Print a copy of your database structure

Database Exercise 2.1

1 Make the database created in Exercise 1 current and edit the file structure to incorporate a field named CONTACT
2 Upon completion, save and print a copy of your database structure

Database Exercise 3

The Sales Director has requested a list of all customers in the database file who have premises in Edinburgh. Search the database for all relevant customers, printing out the customer name and town only

Database Exercise 3.1

1 The following fields require to be added to the database; amend the structure as necessary:

Field Name   Field Type   Field Length

POSITION   Character
ACCOUNT   Numerical   To be decided
TERMS   Numerical
TOTORDER   Numerical

2 Enter the following information in the relevant database records:

Contact: Mr James Smith Jnr
Position: Managing Director
Account No: 00234
Terms: 30 days
Total order to date: £20,045

Contact: Mr P Patterson
Position: Accountant
Account No: 00235
Terms: 30 days
Total order to date: £55,043

Contact: Ms P Burrows
Position: Financial Director
Account No: 00236
Terms: 60 days
Total order to date: £61,050

Contact: Mr Mike Smart
Position: Proprietor
Account No: 00237
Terms: 60 days
Total order to date: £66,000

Contact: Ms L Logan
Position: Accounts Supervisor
Account No: 00238
Terms: 30 days
Total order to date: £80,650

Contact: Ms J Torville
Position: Partner
Account No: 00239
Terms: 30 days
Total order to date: £30,000

Contact: Mr J P Anderson
Position: Managing Director
Account No: 00240
Terms: 30 days
Total order to date: £25,000

Contact: Ms S Swinger
Position: Managing Director
Account No: 00241
Terms: 30 days
Total order to date: £22,000

3 Upon completion, print a copy of your database contents listing only the fields for company name, town, account No, terms and total order to date. Print a copy of your amended file structure

Database Exercise 3.2

1 Search the database for all customers who live in the Aberdeen area in order that a letter informing them of a new promotion taking place in their area may be sent to them. Take a printout of the names and addresses of companies in this area
2 Using an appropriate command, total the sales to date from the Aberdeen area
3 Further records have arrived which require to be input. Key in the following records to your existing database file, listing company, town, terms and total order when printing out

NTP Office Furniture
22 Kingsley Park South
ABERDEEN
AB9 8LL

Contact: Mr D T Smith
Position: Sales Director
Account No: 00242
Terms: 60 days
Total order to date: £55,060

J C Cotters Limited
37 Kingseat Avenue
EDINBURGH
EH7 8JJ

Contact: Mr J C Cotter
Position: Managing Director
Account No: 00424
Terms: 30 days
Total order to date: £21,670

Peters & Smith Fabrics
22 Laurieston Walk
LONDON
NE3

Contact: Mr A P Peters
Position: Sales Director
Account No: 00426
Terms: 30 days
Total order to date: £22,450

Fiona Fashions Limited
36 Highway North
EDINBURGH
ED8 4GH

Contact: Ms Fiona Nicholson
Position: Proprietor
Account No: 00428
Terms: 60 days
Total order to date: £66,327

Anderton & Pauls
34 High Street
GLASGOW
G3 8HH

Contact: Ms A S Pauls
Position: Partner
Account No: 00243
Terms: 60 days
Total order to date: £95,600

Andrew Smith Fashions Ltd
90 Canal Street
EDINBURGH
EH7 9HK

Contact: Ms A Smith
Position: Sales Director
Account No: 00425
Terms: 60 days
Total order to date: £90,050

Allison, Allison
108 Callander Road
LONDON
NW2

Contact: Ms Allison Saunders
Position: Partner
Account No: 00427
Terms: 30 days
Total order to date: £65,320

Baxter & Anderson
58 Oxford Way
LONDON
EC4 8LP

Contact: Mr Andrew Baxter
Position: Partner
Account No: 00429
Terms: 30 days
Total order to date: £16,671

Database Exercise 3.3

1 Search for all customers in Edinburgh with terms of 30 days and order value over £50,000. Print out the company name, town, terms and total order value fields

2 Sort the database into alphabetical order by company. Take a printout of this sorted file, listing company, address and town as the fields to be printed

3 Index the database on town and within town and company, taking a printout listing company, town and account No fields

4 Index the database on order value, printing out on company, town, account No and total order fields

5 Add the following customer record to the database file:

Anderson Brothers (Perth) Ltd
22 High Station Road
PERTH
PE2 8JH

Contact: Ms Paula Anderson
Position: Company Secretary
Account No: 00430
Terms: 60 days
Total order to date: £110,000

6 Delete the following customer records from the database file:

J C Saunder Co Ltd, 21 High Street, EDINBURGH
Jones & Dean PLC, 33 Ice Dr, EDINBURGH

7 The name of the contact at Baxter & Anderson has been changed to Ms Alison Anderson – please amend this record

8 Take a printout of the complete file, selecting the company name, town, account No and contact as the fields to be printed

9 Take a printout of the order value index, printing the fields as per 8 above

10 Take a printout of the sorted database as per step 2 above. Can you see anything wrong with this printout?

Database Exercise 4

1 Make the database created in Exercise 1 current – ie your main database file
2 Customers in London will be transferred to the Southern Regional Office Accounts Department

   1.1 Take a printout of the relevant customer records, listing the fields containing company name, town and account No only
   1.2 Mark for deletion all relevant records, using a search facility to do so, ie do not delete the records individually
   1.3 Take a further printout of this database, listing company name, town and account No only
   1.4 Edit the file structure to include a reference field
   1.5 Locate all customers based in Edinburgh and enter the reference **E**

3 Take a printout listing company name, town and reference only
4 Amend the remaining records using the following references:

   GLASGOW   GLA
   ABERDEEN   AB

5 Key in a command which will locate all customers with the reference **E** and replace this with **EDIN**
6 Edit the records for all customers with terms of 30 days and order values over £50,000 to terms of 60 days, but not London records
7 Print out company name, terms, total order value and reference fields
8 Recall the records previously marked for deletion
9 Print out the contents of your database file, listing company name, town, terms, total order value and reference fields

Database Exercise 4.1

1 Create a report which has the following heading:

CUSTOMER LISTING

Prepared by: Your Name Date: Today's Date

2 Include the following fields, giving appropriate column headings and underscoring these headings:

COMPANY   TOWN   ACCOUNT   TOTORDER   TERMS

3 Total the TOTAL ORDER TO DATE column only
4 The report should be in double line spacing
5 On completion, print a copy of your report

Database Exercise 4.2

1 Sort your database on the town field
2 Make your sorted database current
3 Modify your report created in Database Exercise 4.1, grouping the contents on town, and change to display in single line spacing
4 On completion, print a copy of your modified report

Database Exercise 5

In this exercise you are required to design your own database, taking the following into consideration:

1 The field names should be appropriate to the contents. However, the field name for the Account No should be ACCOUNT
2 The field types should be carefully selected as required – the field type for Account No should be numerical
3 The field lengths should not greatly exceed requirements – the field length for Account No should be equal to the previous database length for this field
4 On completion, take a printout of your database structure

Database Exercise 5.1

1 Key in the following information:

ACCOUNT NO	NEW ORDERS	DATE	REPRESENTATIVE
00428	£1,500	03/03/—	Patterson, Douglas
00235	£3,500	05/07/—	Thomson, Danielle
00236	£5,000	03/03/—	Smith, Harry
00237	£2,350	01/03/—	Sommerville, Alison
00238	£2,300	01/03/—	Thomson, Danielle
00242	£2,500	01/04/—	Thomson, Danielle
00243	£5,000	10/04/—	Smith, Harry
00424	£2,000	10/04/—	Sommerville, Alison
00425	£1,200	30/04/—	Patterson, Douglas
00428	£800	30/04/—	Patterson, Douglas
00430	£5,300	01/05/—	Smith, Harry

2 Prepare an appropriate report format, grouping on the field containing the Representative's name

Database Exercise 6

1 Join the database created in Exercise 1 to the database created in Exercise 5, using the ACCOUNT field as the common link, and selecting the fields COMPANY, ACCOUNT, NEW ORDERS and TOTORDER
2 Print out both the contents and file structure of this database

Database Exercise 7

1 Make the database created in Exercise 5 current
2 Convert the contents of this database to a format which could be read by a text processing program
3 Take a printout of this file using the appropriate text processing program

Database Exercise 8

1 Make the database created in Exercise 1 current
2 Convert the contents of this database to a format which could be read by a text processing program
3 Take a printout of this file, using the appropriate text processing program

Database Exercise 9

1 Make a security copy of your database files created in Exercise 1 and Exercise 2, naming them Ex1bak and Ex2bak
2 Take a printout of the relevant file directory displaying the back-up files.

Database Exercise 10

Design and enter the following information into a database file, allocating field names, field lengths, types, etc, as necessary.

Author	Title	Publisher	In Stock
Alibert, P	Marketing Now	Smitherson Press	15
Smith, JC	The Marketing Age	Smitherson Press	7
Pauls, PT	Computing Today	P J Thomson	2
Andrews, J	Effective Communications	Putney Publications	7
Thomson, AT	The Computing Age	Putney Publications	10
McQueen, K	Alcohol at Work	Putney Publications	2
McDonald, T	Effective Operations Management	Smitherson Press	10
Passion, TJ	The New Manager	P J Thomson	5
Baxter, D	Managing Change	Smitherson Press	12
Carruthers, S	Assertiveness	Putney Publications	15
Patterson, TD	Introducing Computing	Putney Publications	7
Hendry, J	Compute-it	Smitherson Press	13
Koszary, B	Safety Now	Putney Publications	12
Rae, A	Administrative Procedures	Smitherson Press	9
Ross, T	Mechanics for Today	P J Thomson	12
Graham, D	Computerised Stock	Putney Publications	10
Steel, S	Hairdressing for the 90's	Smitherson Press	2
Rae, A	Introducing Spreadsheets	Putney Publications	10
Rae, A	Introducing Database	Putney Publications	10
Rae, A	Word Processing for Beginners	Putney Publications	12
Koszary, B	Safety and Youth	Putney Publications	15
Baxter, D	Spreadsheets for Managers	Smitherson Press	9
Hendry, J	Computing for Beginners	Smitherson Press	12
Passion, TJ	The Manager and Me	P J Thomson	15
Bassey, S	Administering Change	P J Thomson	16

165

Database Exercise 10.1

You are required to carry out the following searches on the database contents, taking printouts as you carry out each task:

1 Carry out a partial search on all books containing **Comp** (short for computing) in their title
2 Search for all books on **Spreadsheets**
3 You require to complete your reorder invoice and wish to have a list of all books with a stock less than or equal to **10**
4 You wish to know the details of all books currently held in stock for the publisher **Smitherson Press**
5 You require to have a list of all publications by the author **A Rae**
6 You need to total the stock held on the author **A Rae** as well as on the authors **J Hendry** and **T J Passion**
7 You need to have the total of all books currently held in stock

Database Exercise 10.2

You require to sort the database for future use:

1 Sort the database on Publisher, taking a printout
2 Sort the database on Author, taking a printout
3 Using the INDEX function, index the database primarily by publisher and secondly by author
4 Take a printout in REPORT FORMAT of this indexed database

Database Exercise 11

Enter the following information in a database file, allocating the field names as appropriate. Please use the same field name, type and size for the Title field as used when creating your database in Exercise 10.

Title	In Stock	Min Stock
Marketing Now	15	5
The Marketing Age	7	10
Computing Today	2	5
Effective Communications	7	10
The Computing Age	10	12
Alcohol at Work	2	5
Effective Operations Management	10	12
The New Manager	5	7
Managing Change	12	10
Assertiveness	15	10
Introducing Computing	7	10
Compute-it	13	10
Safety Now	12	9
Administrative Procedures	9	5
Mechanics for Today	12	10
Computerised Stock	10	10
Hairdressing for the 90's	2	5
Introducing Spreadsheets	10	10
Introducing Database	10	10
Word Processing for Beginners	12	10
Safety and Youth	15	10
Spreadsheets for Managers	9	10
Computing for Beginners	12	10
The Manager and Me	15	9
Administering Change	16	5

Database Exercise 11.1

You are now required to join the databases created in Exercises 10 and 11 on the Title field and incorporating:

Author, Title and In Stock fields from Exercise 10
Title and Min Stock fields from Exercise 11

Take a printout of the file structure.

Database Exercise 11.2

You should make your joined database current in order to carry out this exercise.

1 Index the database on author
2 Create a report incorporating the following information:

   (a) The author's name
   (b) The book title
   (c) The quantity in stock
   (d) The minimum stock quantity
   (e) The reorder quantity (ie minimum stock less quantity in stock)

3 Delete the following records from your file:

   Alcohol at Work
   Administrative Procedures
   Computerised Stock
   Introducing Database
   Word Processing for Beginners
4 On completion, run a print of this report.

Database solutions

Database Exercise 1

Record£	COMPANY	ADDRESS1	TOWN	POSTCODE
1	Saunder J C Co Ltd	21 High St	EDINBURGH	EH2 5HH
2	Burrows A & P	23 Anderston Dr	ABERDEEN	AB6 7BZ
3	Alderton & Simms Ltd	33 Ashton Rd	EDINBURGH	EH5 5QQ
4	Thomson & Co	57 High St	ABERDEEN	AB1 1JT
5	Andrews Bros	55 North Byers Rd	ABERDEEN	AB6 4PT
6	Curtain Call	23 Coronation St	EDINBURGH	EH2 7HB
7	Jones & Dean PLC	33 Ice Drive	EDINBURGH	EH3 2NJ
8	Peebles Fashions Ltd	33 Mottles Green	LONDON	NW4

```
Structure for database: A:ex1.dbf
Number of data records:        8
Date of last update   : 01/01/
```

Field	Field Name	Type	Width	Dec
1	COMPANY	Character	20	
2	ADDRESS1	Character	20	
3	TOWN	Character	15	
4	POSTCODE	Character	8	
** Total **			64	

Database Exercise 2

Record£	NAME	POSITION	START_DATE	PAY
1	Andrews, Alex	Supervisor	03/09/70	16252
2	Smith James	Asst Manager	15/10/75	18000
3	Sneddon Pauline	Secretary	22/03/72	13500
4	Smith Andrew	Clerk	22/04/68	10025
5	Drummond Alison	Clerk	17/04/85	6900
6	McLean Vivien	Wages Clerk	21/01/88	7200
7	Duncan David	Manager	20/07/69	20000

```
Structure for database: A:ex2.dbf
Number of data records:        7
Date of last update   : 01/01/
```

Field	Field Name	Type	Width	Dec
1	NAME	Character	20	
2	POSITION	Character	15	
3	START_DATE	Date	8	
4	PAY	Numeric	6	
** Total **			50	

Database Exercise 2.1

```
Structure for database: A:ex1.dbf
Number of data records:       8
Date of last update   : 01/01/
Field  Field Name  Type        Width    Dec
    1  COMPANY     Character     20
    2  ADDRESS1    Character     20
    3  TOWN        Character     15
    4  POSTCODE    Character      8
    5  CONTACT     Character     15
** Total **                     79
```

Database Exercise 3

```
Record£  COMPANY              TOWN
      1  Saunder J C Co Ltd   EDINBURGH
      3  Alderton & Simms Ltd EDINBURGH
      6  Curtain Call         EDINBURGH
      7  Jones & Dean PLC     EDINBURGH
```

Database Exercise 3.1

```
Record£  company              town        account terms  tot_order
      1  Saunder J C Co Ltd   EDINBURGH      234    30       20045
      2  Burrows A & P        ABERDEEN       236    60       61050
      3  Alderton & Simms Ltd EDINBURGH      238    30       80650
      4  Thomson & Co         ABERDEEN       240    30       25000
      5  Andrews Bros         ABERDEEN       235    30       55043
      6  Curtain Call         EDINBURGH      237    60       66000
      7  Jones & Dean PLC     EDINBURGH      239    30       30000
      8  Peebles Fashions Ltd LONDON         241    30       22000
```

```
Structure for database: A:ex1.dbf
Number of data records:       8
Date of last update   : 01/01/
Field  Field Name  Type       Width   Dec
    1  COMPANY     Character    20
    2  ADDRESS1    Character    20
    3  TOWN        Character    15
    4  POSTCODE    Character     8
    5  CONTACT     Character    20
    6  POSITION    Character    20
    7  ACCOUNT     Numeric       5
    8  TERMS       Numeric       2
    9  TOT_ORDER   Numeric       6
** Total **                    117
```

Database Exercise 3.2 (1)

Record£	company	address1	town
2	Burrows A & P	23 Anderston Dr	ABERDEEN
4	Thomson & Co	57 High St	ABERDEEN
5	Andrews Bros	55 North Byers Rd	ABERDEEN

Database Exercise 3.2 (2)

```
    3 records summed
TOT_ORDER
    141093
```

Database Exercise 3.2 (3)

Record£	company	town	terms	tot_order
1	Saunder J C Co Ltd	EDINBURGH	30	20045
2	Burrows A & P	ABERDEEN	60	61050
3	Alderton & Simms Ltd	EDINBURGH	30	80650
4	Thomson & Co	ABERDEEN	30	25000
5	Andrews Bros	ABERDEEN	30	55043
6	Curtain Call	EDINBURGH	60	66000
7	Jones & Dean PLC	EDINBURGH	30	30000
8	Peebles Fashions Ltd	LONDON	30	22000
9	NTP Office Furniture	ABERDEEN	60	55060
10	Cotters J C Ltd	EDINBURGH	30	21670
11	Peters & Smith Fabrics	LONDON	30	22450
12	Fiona Fashions Ltd	EDINBURGH	60	66327
13	Anderton & Pauls	GLASGOW	60	95600
14	Smith Andrew Fashions Ltd	EDINBURGH	60	90050
15	Allison Allison	LONDON	30	65320
16	Baxter & Anderson	LONDON	30	16671

Database Exercise 3.3 (1)

Record£	company	town	terms	tot_order
3	Alderton & Simms Ltd	EDINBURGH	30	80650

Database Exercise 3.3 (2)

Record£	company	ADDRESS1	town
1	Alderton & Simms Ltd	33 Ashton Rd	EDINBURGH
2	Allison Allison	108 Callander Rd	LONDON
3	Anderton & Pauls	34 High St	GLASGOW
4	Andrews Bros	55 North Byers Rd	ABERDEEN
5	Baxter & Anderson	56 Oxford Way	LONDON
6	Burrows A & P	23 Anderston Dr	ABERDEEN
7	Cotters J C Ltd	37 Kingseat Ave	EDINBURGH
8	Curtain Call	23 Coronation St	EDINBURGH
9	Fiona Fashions Ltd	36 Highway North	EDINBURGH
10	Jones & Dean PLC	33 Ice Drive	EDINBURGH
11	NTP Office Furniture	22 Kingsley Park Sth	ABERDEEN
12	Peebles Fashions Ltd	33 Mottles Green	LONDON
13	Peters & Smith Fabrics	22 Laurieston Walk	LONDON
14	Saunder J C Co Ltd	21 High St	EDINBURGH
15	Smith Andrew Fashions Ltd	90 Canal St	EDINBURGH
16	Thomson & Co	57 High St	ABERDEEN

Database Exercise 3.3 (3)

Record£	COMPANY	TOWN	ACCOUNT
5	Andrews Bros	ABERDEEN	235
2	Burrows A & P	ABERDEEN	236
9	NTP Office Furniture	ABERDEEN	242
4	Thomson & Co	ABERDEEN	240
3	Alderton & Simms Ltd	EDINBURGH	238
10	Cotters J C Ltd	EDINBURGH	424
6	Curtain Call	EDINBURGH	237
12	Fiona Fashions Ltd	EDINBURGH	428
7	Jones & Dean PLC	EDINBURGH	239
1	Saunder J C Co Ltd	EDINBURGH	234
14	Smith Andrew Fashions Ltd	EDINBURGH	425
13	Anderton & Pauls	GLASGOW	243
15	Allison Allison	LONDON	427
16	Baxter & Anderson	LONDON	429
8	Peebles Fashions Ltd	LONDON	241
11	Peters & Smith Fabrics	LONDON	426

Database Exercise 3.3 (4)

Record£	COMPANY	TOWN	ACCOUNT	TOT_ORDER
16	Baxter & Anderson	LONDON	429	16671
1	Saunder J C Co Ltd	EDINBURGH	234	20045
10	Cotters J C Ltd	EDINBURGH	424	21670
8	Peebles Fashions Ltd	LONDON	241	22000
11	Peters & Smith Fabrics	LONDON	426	22450
4	Thomson & Co	ABERDEEN	240	25000
7	Jones & Dean PLC	EDINBURGH	239	30000
5	Andrews Bros	ABERDEEN	235	55043
9	NTP Office Furniture	ABERDEEN	242	55060
2	Burrows A & P	ABERDEEN	236	61050
15	Allison Allison	LONDON	427	65320
6	Curtain Call	EDINBURGH	237	66000
12	Fiona Fashions Ltd	EDINBURGH	428	66327
3	Alderton & Simms Ltd	EDINBURGH	238	80650
14	Smith Andrew Fashions Ltd	EDINBURGH	425	90050
13	Anderton & Pauls	GLASGOW	243	95600

Database Exercise 3.3 (5)

Record£	COMPANY	TOWN	ACCOUNT	CONTACT
1	Burrows A & P	ABERDEEN	236	Ms P Burrows
2	Alderton & Simms Ltd	EDINBURGH	238	Ms L Logan
3	Thomson & Co	ABERDEEN	240	Mr J P Anderson
4	Andrews Bros	ABERDEEN	235	Mr P Patterson
5	Curtain Call	EDINBURGH	237	Mr Mike Smart
6	Peebles Fashions Ltd	LONDON	241	Ms S Swinger
7	NTP Office Furniture	ABERDEEN	242	Mr D T Smith
8	Cotters J C Ltd	EDINBURGH	424	Mr J C Cotter
9	Peters & Smith Fabrics	LONDON	426	Mr A P Peters
10	Fiona Fashions Ltd	EDINBURGH	428	Ms Fiona Nicholson
11	Anderton & Pauls	GLASGOW	243	Ms A S Pauls
12	Smith Andrew Fashions Ltd	EDINBURGH	425	Ms A Smith
13	Allison Allison	LONDON	427	Ms Allison Saunders
14	Baxter & Anderson	LONDON	429	Ms Alison Anderson
15	Anderson Bros (Perth) Ltd	PERTH	430	Ms Paula Anderson

Database Exercise 3.3 (6)

Record£	COMPANY	TOWN	ACCOUNT	TERMS	TOT_ORDER
14	Baxter & Anderson	LONDON	429	30	16671
8	Cotters J C Ltd	EDINBURGH	424	30	21670
6	Peebles Fashions Ltd	LONDON	241	30	22000
9	Peters & Smith Fabrics	LONDON	426	30	22450
3	Thomson & Co	ABERDEEN	240	30	25000
4	Andrews Bros	ABERDEEN	235	30	55043
7	NTP Office Furniture	ABERDEEN	242	60	55060
1	Burrows A & P	ABERDEEN	236	60	61050
13	Allison Allison	LONDON	427	30	65320
5	Curtain Call	EDINBURGH	237	60	66000
10	Fiona Fashions Ltd	EDINBURGH	428	60	66327
2	Alderton & Simms Ltd	EDINBURGH	238	30	80650
12	Smith Andrew Fashions Ltd	EDINBURGH	425	60	90050
11	Anderton & Pauls	GLASGOW	243	60	95600
15	Anderson Bros (Perth) Ltd	PERTH	430	60	110000

Database Exercise 3.3 (7)

Record£	COMPANY	ADDRESS1	TOWN
1	Alderton & Simms Ltd	33 Ashton Rd	EDINBURGH
2	Allison Allison	108 Callander Rd	LONDON
3	Anderton & Pauls	34 High St	GLASGOW
4	Andrews Bros	55 North Byers Rd	ABERDEEN
5	Baxter & Anderson	56 Oxford Way	LONDON
6	Burrows A & P	23 Anderston Dr	ABERDEEN
7	Cotters J C Ltd	37 Kingseat Ave	EDINBURGH
8	Curtain Call	23 Coronation St	EDINBURGH
9	Fiona Fashions Ltd	36 Highway North	EDINBURGH
10	Jones & Dean PLC	33 Ice Drive	EDINBURGH
11	NTP Office Furniture	22 Kingsley Park Sth	ABERDEEN
12	Peebles Fashions Ltd	33 Mottles Green	LONDON
13	Peters & Smith Fabrics	22 Laurieston Walk	LONDON
14	Saunder J C Co Ltd	21 High St	EDINBURGH
15	Smith Andrew Fashions Ltd	90 Canal St	EDINBURGH
16	Thomson & Co	57 High St	ABERDEEN

Answer

The additions, deletions and edits are missing but are present in the index. That is why it is often better to use indexed files rather than to sort to a new file.

Database Exercise 4 (1)

Record£	company	town	account
6	Peebles Fashions Ltd	LONDON	241
9	Peters & Smith Fabrics	LONDON	426
13	Allison Allison	LONDON	427
14	Baxter & Anderson	LONDON	429

Database Exercise 4 (2)

Record£	COMPANY	TOWN	ACCOUNT
1	Burrows A & P	ABERDEEN	236
2	Alderton & Simms Ltd	EDINBURGH	238
3	Thomson & Co	ABERDEEN	240
4	Andrews Bros	ABERDEEN	235
5	Curtain Call	EDINBURGH	237
6	*Peebles Fashions Ltd	LONDON	241
7	NTP Office Furniture	ABERDEEN	242
8	Cotters J C Ltd	EDINBURGH	424
9	*Peters & Smith Fabrics	LONDON	426
10	Fiona Fashions Ltd	EDINBURGH	428
11	Anderton & Pauls	GLASGOW	243
12	Smith Andrew Fashions Ltd	EDINBURGH	425
13	*Allison Allison	LONDON	427
14	*Baxter & Anderson	LONDON	429
15	Anderson Bros (Perth) Ltd	PERTH	430

Database Exercise 4 (3)

Record£	COMPANY	TOWN	REFERENCE
1	Burrows A & P	ABERDEEN	
2	Alderton & Simms Ltd	EDINBURGH	E
3	Thomson & Co	ABERDEEN	
4	Andrews Bros	ABERDEEN	
5	Curtain Call	EDINBURGH	E
6	*Peebles Fashions Ltd	LONDON	
7	NTP Office Furniture	ABERDEEN	
8	Cotters J C Ltd	EDINBURGH	E
9	*Peters & Smith Fabrics	LONDON	
10	Fiona Fashions Ltd	EDINBURGH	E
11	Anderton & Pauls	GLASGOW	
12	Smith Andrew Fashions Ltd	EDINBURGH	E
13	*Allison Allison	LONDON	
14	*Baxter & Anderson	LONDON	
15	Anderson Bros (Perth) Ltd	PERTH	

Database Exercise 4 (4)

Record£	COMPANY	TERMS	TOT_ORDER	REFERENCE
1	Burrows A & P	60	61050	AB
2	Alderton & Simms Ltd	60	80650	EDIN
3	Thomson & Co	30	25000	AB
4	Andrews Bros	60	55043	AB
5	Curtain Call	60	66000	EDIN
6	*Peebles Fashions Ltd	30	22000	
7	NTP Office Furniture	60	55060	AB
8	Cotters J C Ltd	30	21670	EDIN
9	*Peters & Smith Fabrics	30	22450	
10	Fiona Fashions Ltd	60	66327	EDIN
11	Anderton & Pauls	60	95600	GLA
12	Smith Andrew Fashions Ltd	60	90050	EDIN
13	*Allison Allison	60	65320	
14	*Baxter & Anderson	30	16671	
15	Anderson Bros (Perth) Ltd	60	110000	

Database Exercise 4 (5)

Record£	COMPANY	TOWN	TERMS	TOT_ORDER	REFERENCE
1	Burrows A & P	ABERDEEN	60	61050	AB
2	Alderton & Simms Ltd	EDINBURGH	60	80650	EDIN
3	Thomson & Co	ABERDEEN	30	25000	AB
4	Andrews Bros	ABERDEEN	60	55043	AB
5	Curtain Call	EDINBURGH	60	66000	EDIN
6	Peebles Fashions Ltd	LONDON	30	22000	
7	NTP Office Furniture	ABERDEEN	60	55060	AB
8	Cotters J C Ltd	EDINBURGH	30	21670	EDIN
9	Peters & Smith Fabrics	LONDON	30	22450	
10	Fiona Fashions Ltd	EDINBURGH	60	66327	EDIN
11	Anderton & Pauls	GLASGOW	60	95600	GLA
12	Smith Andrew Fashions Ltd	EDINBURGH	60	90050	EDIN
13	Allison Allison	LONDON	60	65320	
14	Baxter & Anderson	LONDON	30	16671	
15	Anderson Bros (Perth) Ltd	PERTH	60	110000	

Database Exercise 4.1

Page No.   1
01/01/
CUSTOMER LISTING

Prepared by: Elizabeth A Rae   Date: Today's Date

COMPANY NAME	TOWN	ACCOUNT NUMBER	ORDER VALUE	TERMS
------------	----	------	-----	-----
Burrows A & P	ABERDEEN	236	61050	60
Alderton & Simms Ltd	EDINBURGH	238	80650	60
Thomson & Co	ABERDEEN	240	25000	30
Andrews Bros	ABERDEEN	235	55043	60
Curtain Call	EDINBURGH	237	66000	60
Peebles Fashions Ltd	LONDON	241	22000	30
NTP Office Furniture	ABERDEEN	242	55060	60
Cotters J C Ltd	EDINBURGH	424	21670	30
Peters & Smith Fabrics	LONDON	426	22450	30
Fiona Fashions Ltd	EDINBURGH	428	66327	60
Anderton & Pauls	GLASGOW	243	95600	60
Smith Andrew Fashions Ltd	EDINBURGH	425	90050	60
Allison Allison	LONDON	427	65320	60
Baxter & Anderson	LONDON	429	16671	30
Anderson Bros (Perth) Ltd	PERTH	430	110000	60

*** Total ***

852891

Database Exercise 4.2

                          CUSTOMER LISTING

          Prepared by: Elizabeth A Rae   Date: Today's Date

COMPANY NAME	TOWN	ACCOUNT NUMBER	ORDER VALUE	TERMS
------------	----	------	-----	-----
** BASE TOWN ABERDEEN				
Burrows A & P	ABERDEEN	236	61050	60
Thomson & Co	ABERDEEN	240	25000	30
Andrews Bros	ABERDEEN	235	55043	60
NTP Office Furniture	ABERDEEN	242	55060	60
** Subtotal **				
			196153	
** BASE TOWN EDINBURGH				
Alderton & Simms Ltd	EDINBURGH	238	80650	60
Curtain Call	EDINBURGH	237	66000	60
Cotters J C Ltd	EDINBURGH	424	21670	30
Fiona Fashions Ltd	EDINBURGH	428	66327	60
Smith Andrew Fashions Ltd	EDINBURGH	425	90050	60
** Subtotal **				
			324697	
** BASE TOWN GLASGOW				
Anderton & Pauls	GLASGOW	243	95600	60
** Subtotal **				
			95600	
** BASE TOWN LONDON				
Peebles Fashions Ltd	LONDON	241	22000	30
Peters & Smith Fabrics	LONDON	426	22450	30
Allison Allison	LONDON	427	65320	60
Baxter & Anderson	LONDON	429	16671	30
** Subtotal **				
			126441	
** BASE TOWN PERTH				
Anderson Bros (Perth) Ltd	PERTH	430	110000	60
** Subtotal **				
			110000	
*** Total ***				
			852891	

Database Exercise 5

```
Structure for database: A:ACCOUNTS.dbf
Number of data records:        11
Date of last update   : 01/01/
Field  Field Name  Type       Width    Dec
    1  ACCOUNT     Numeric        5
    2  NEW_ORDERS  Numeric        6
    3  DATE        Date           8
    4  REP         Character     19
**  Total  **                    39
```

Database Exercise 5.1

NEW BUSINESS
REPORT

Prepared by: Elizabeth A Rae   Date: Today's Date

ACCOUNT NUMBER	ORDER VALUE	DATE OF ORDER
-------	-----	-------

** REPRESENTATIVE Patterson Douglas

428	1500	03/03/91
425	1200	30/04/91
428	800	30/04/91

** Subtotal **

3500

** REPRESENTATIVE Smith Harry

236	5000	03/03/91
243	5000	10/04/91
430	5300	01/05/91

** Subtotal **

15300

** REPRESENTATIVE Sommerville Alison

237	2350	01/03/91
424	2000	10/04/91

** Subtotal **

4350

** REPRESENTATIVE Thomson Danielle

235	3500	05/07/91
238	2300	01/03/91
242	2500	01/04/91

** Subtotal **

8300

*** Total ***

31450

Database Exercise 6

```
Structure for database: A:EX6.dbf
Number of data records:        11
Date of last update   : 01/01/
Field   Field Name   Type        Width     Dec
   1    ACCOUNT      Numeric         5
   2    COMPANY      Character      25
   3    NEW_ORDERS   Numeric         6
   4    TOT_ORDER    Numeric         6
** Total **                        43
```

Record#	ACCOUNT	COMPANY	NEW_ORDERS	TOT_ORDER
1	236	Burrows A & P	5000	61050
2	238	Alderton & Simms Ltd	2300	80650
3	235	Andrews Bros	3500	55043
4	237	Curtain Call	2350	66000
5	242	NTP Office Furniture	2500	55060
6	424	Cotters J C Ltd	2000	21670
7	428	Fiona Fashions Ltd	1500	66327
8	428	Fiona Fashions Ltd	800	66327
9	243	Anderton & Pauls	5000	95600
10	425	Smith Andrew Fashions Ltd	1200	90050
11	430	Anderson Bros (Perth) Ltd	5300	110000

Database Exercise 7

```
428,1500,19910303,"Patterson Douglas"
235,3500,19910705,"Thomson Danielle"
236,5000,19910303,"Smith Harry"
237,2350,19910301,"Sommerville Alison"
238,2300,19910301,"Thomson Danielle"
242,2500,19910401,"Thomson Danielle"
243,5000,19910410,"Smith Harry"
424,2000,19910410,"Sommerville Alison"
425,1200,19910430,"Patterson Douglas"
428,800,19910430,"Patterson Douglas"
430,5300,19910501,"Smith Harry"
```

Database Exercise 8

"Burrows A & P","23 Anderston Dr","ABERDEEN","AB6 7BZ","Ms P Burrows","Financial Director",236,60,61050,"EDIN"
"Alderton & Simms Ltd","33 Ashton Rd","EDINBURGH","EH5 5QQ","Ms L Logan","Accounts Supervisor",238,60,80650,"EDIN"
"Thomson & Co","57 High St","ABERDEEN","AB1 1JT","Mr J P anderson","Managing Director",240,30,25000,"AB"
"Andrews Bros","55 North Byers Rd","ABERDEEN","AB6 4PT","Mr P Patterson","Accountant",235,60,55043,"AB"
"Curtain Call","23 Coronation St","EDINBURGH","EH2 7HB","Mr Mike Smart","Proprietor",237,60,66000,"EDIN"
"Peebles Fashions Ltd","33 Mottles Green","LONDON","NW4","Ms S Swinger","Managing Director",241,30,22000,""
"NTP Office Furniture","22 Kingsley Park Sth","ABERDEEN","AB9 8LL","Mr D T Smith","Sales Director",242,6,55060,"AB"
"Cotters J C Ltd","37 Kingseat Ave","EDINBURGH","EH7 8JJ","Mr J C Cotter","Managing Director",424,3,21670,"EDIN"
"Peters & Smith Fabrics","22 Laurieston Walk","LONDON","NE3","Mr A P Peters","Sales Director",426,30,22450,""
"Fiona Fashions Ltd","36 Highway North","EDINBURGH","EH8 4GH","Ms Fiona Nicholson","Proprietor",428,60,66327,"EDIN"
"Anderton & Pauls","34 High St","GLASGOW","G3 8HH","Ms A S Pauls","Partner",243,60,95600,"GLA"
"Smith Andrew Fashions Ltd","90 Canal St","EDINBURGH","EH7 9HK","Ms A Smith","Sales Director",425,60,90050,"EDIN"
"Allison Allison","108 Callander Rd","LONDON","NW2","Ms Allison Saunders","Partner",427,60,65320,""
"Baxter & Anderson","56 Oxford Way","LONDON","EC4 8LP","Ms Alison Anderson","Partner",429,30,16671,""
"Anderson Bros (Perth) Ltd","22 High Station Rd","PERTH","PE2 8JH","Ms Paula Anderson","Company Secretary",430,60,110000,""

Database Exercise 10

Record#	AUTHOR	TITLE	PUBLISHER	INSTOCK
1	ALIBERT, P	MARKETING NOW	SMITHERSON PRESS	15
2	SMITH, JC	THE MARKETING AGE	SMITHERSON PRESS	7
3	PAULS, PT	COMPUTING TODAY	P J THOMSON	2
4	ANDREWS, J	EFFECTIVE COMMUNICATIONS	PUTNEY PUBLICATIONS	7
5	THOMSON, AT	THE COMPUTING AGE	PUTNEY PUBLICATIONS	10
6	MCQUEEN, K	ALCOHOL AT WORK	PUTNEY PUBLICATIONS	2
7	MCDONALD, T	EFFECTIVE OPERATIONS MANAGEMENT	SMITHERSON PRESS	10
8	PASSION, TJ	THE NEW MANAGER	P J THOMSON	5
9	BAXTER, D	MANAGING CHANGE	SMITHERSON PRESS	12
10	CARRUTHERS, S	ASSERTIVENESS	PUTNEY PUBLICATIONS	15
11	PATTERSON, TD	INTRODUCING COMPUTING	PUTNEY PUBLICATIONS	7
12	HENDRY, J	COMPUTE-IT	SMITHERSON PRESS	13
13	KOSZARY, B	SAFETY NOW	PUTNEY PUBLICATIONS	1
14	RAE, A	ADMINISTRATIVE PROCEDURES	SMITHERSON PRESS	9
15	ROSS, T	MECHANICS FOR TODAY	P J THOMSON	12
16	GRAHAM, D	COMPUTERISED STOCK	PUTNEY PUBLICATIONS	10
17	STEEL, S	HAIRDRESSING FOR THE 90'S	SMITHERSON PRESS	2
18	RAE, A	INTRODUCING SPREADSHEETS	PUTNEY PUBLICATIONS	10
19	RAE, A	INTRODUCING DATABASE	PUTNEY PUBLICATIONS	10
20	RAE, A	WORD PROCESSING FOR BEGINNERS	PUTNEY PUBLICATIONS	12
21	KOSZARY, B	SAFETY AND YOUTH	PUTNEY PUBLICATIONS	15
22	BAXTER, D	SPREADSHEETS FOR MANAGERS	SMITHERSON PRESS	9
23	HENDRY, J	COMPUTING FOR BEGINNERS	SMITHERSON PRESS	12
24	PASSION, TJ	THE MANAGER AND ME	P J THOMSON	15
25	BASSEY, S	ADMINISTERING CHANGE	P J THOMSON	16

Database Exercise 10.1 (1)

Record#	AUTHOR	TITLE	PUBLISHER	INSTOCK
3	PAULS, PT	COMPUTING TODAY	P J THOMSON	2
5	THOMSON, AT	THE COMPUTING AGE	PUTNEY PUBLICATIONS	10
11	PATTERSON, TD	INTRODUCING COMPUTING	PUTNEY PUBLICATIONS	7
12	HENDRY, J	COMPUTE-IT	SMITHERSON PRESS	13
16	GRAHAM, D	COMPUTERISED STOCK	PUTNEY PUBLICATIONS	10
23	HENDRY, J	COMPUTING FOR BEGINNERS	SMITHERSON PRESS	12

Database Exercise 10.1 (2)

Record#	AUTHOR	TITLE	PUBLISHER	INSTOCK
18	RAE, A	INTRODUCING SPREADSHEETS	PUTNEY PUBLICATIONS	10
22	BAXTER, D	SPREADSHEETS FOR MANAGERS	SMITHERSON PRESS	9

Database Exercise 10.1 (3)

Record#	AUTHOR	TITLE	PUBLISHER	INSTOCK
2	SMITH, JC	THE MARKETING AGE	SMITHERSON PRESS	7
3	PAULS, PT	COMPUTING TODAY	P J THOMSON	2
4	ANDREWS, J	EFFECTIVE COMMUNICATIONS	PUTNEY PUBLICATIONS	7
5	THOMSON, AT	THE COMPUTING AGE	PUTNEY PUBLICATIONS	10
6	MCQUEEN, K	ALCOHOL AT WORK	PUTNEY PUBLICATIONS	2
7	MCDONALD, T	EFFECTIVE OPERATIONS MANAGEMENT	SMITHERSON PRESS	10
8	PASSION, TJ	THE NEW MANAGER	P J THOMSON	5
11	PATTERSON, TD	INTRODUCING COMPUTING	PUTNEY PUBLICATIONS	7
13	KOSZARY, B	SAFETY NOW	PUTNEY PUBLICATIONS	1
14	RAE, A	ADMINISTRATIVE PROCEDURES	SMITHERSON PRESS	9
16	GRAHAM, D	COMPUTERISED STOCK	PUTNEY PUBLICATIONS	10
17	STEEL, S	HAIRDRESSING FOR THE 90'S	SMITHERSON PRESS	2
18	RAE, A	INTRODUCING SPREADSHEETS	PUTNEY PUBLICATIONS	10
19	RAE, A	INTRODUCING DATABASE	PUTNEY PUBLICATIONS	10
22	BAXTER, D	SPREADSHEETS FOR MANAGERS	SMITHERSON PRESS	9

Database Exercise 10.1 (4)

Record#	AUTHOR	TITLE	PUBLISHER	INSTOCK
1	ALIBERT, P	MARKETING NOW	SMITHERSON PRESS	15
2	SMITH, JC	THE MARKETING AGE	SMITHERSON PRESS	7
7	MCDONALD, T	EFFECTIVE OPERATIONS MANAGEMENT	SMITHERSON PRESS	10
9	BAXTER, D	MANAGING CHANGE	SMITHERSON PRESS	12
12	HENDRY, J	COMPUTE-IT	SMITHERSON PRESS	13
14	RAE, A	ADMINISTRATIVE PROCEDURES	SMITHERSON PRESS	9
17	STEEL, S	HAIRDRESSING FOR THE 90'S	SMITHERSON PRESS	2
22	BAXTER, D	SPREADSHEETS FOR MANAGERS	SMITHERSON PRESS	9
23	HENDRY, J	COMPUTING FOR BEGINNERS	SMITHERSON PRESS	12

Database Exercise 10.1 (5)

Record#	AUTHOR	TITLE	PUBLISHER	INSTOCK
14	RAE, A	ADMINISTRATIVE PROCEDURES	SMITHERSON PRESS	9
18	RAE, A	INTRODUCING SPREADSHEETS	PUTNEY PUBLICATIONS	10
19	RAE, A	INTRODUCING DATABASE	PUTNEY PUBLICATIONS	10
20	RAE, A	WORD PROCESSING FOR BEGINNERS	PUTNEY PUBLICATIONS	12

Database Exercise 10.1 (6)

```
        SUM INSTOCK FOR AUTHOR='RAE, A'
   4 records summed
INSTOCK
     41



        SUM INSTOCK FOR AUTHOR='HENDRY, J'
   2 records summed
INSTOCK
     25



        SUM INSTOCK FOR AUTHOR='PASSION, TJ'
   2 records summed
INSTOCK
     20
```

Database Exercise 10.1 (7)

```
        SUM INSTOCK
  25 records summed
INSTOCK
    238
```

Database Exercise 10.2 (1)

Record£	AUTHOR	TITLE	PUBLISHER	INSTOCK
1	PASSION, TJ	THE NEW MANAGER	P J THOMSON	5
2	BASSEY, S	ADMINISTERING CHANGE	P J THOMSON	16
3	PASSION, TJ	THE MANAGER AND ME	P J THOMSON	15
4	PAULS, PT	COMPUTING TODAY	P J THOMSON	2
5	ROSS, T	MECHANICS FOR TODAY	P J THOMSON	12
6	MCQUEEN, K	ALCOHOL AT WORK	PUTNEY PUBLICATIONS	2
7	KOSZARY, B	SAFETY AND YOUTH	PUTNEY PUBLICATIONS	15
8	ANDREWS, J	EFFECTIVE COMMUNICATIONS	PUTNEY PUBLICATIONS	7
9	THOMSON, AT	THE COMPUTING AGE	PUTNEY PUBLICATIONS	10
10	CARRUTHERS,S	ASSERTIVENESS	PUTNEY PUBLICATIONS	15
11	PATTERSON,TD	INTRODUCING COMPUTING	PUTNEY PUBLICATIONS	7
12	RAE, A	INTRODUCING DATABASE	PUTNEY PUBLICATIONS	10
13	RAE, A	INTRODUCING SPREADSHEETS	PUTNEY PUBLICATIONS	10
14	GRAHAM, D	COMPUTERISED STOCK	PUTNEY PUBLICATIONS	10
15	RAE, A	WORD PROCESSING FOR BEGINNERS	PUTNEY PUBLICATIONS	12
16	KOSZARY, B	SAFETY NOW	PUTNEY PUBLICATIONS	1
17	STEEL, S	HAIRDRESSING FOR THE 90'S	SMITHERSON PRESS	2
18	RAE, A	ADMINISTRATIVE PROCEDURES	SMITHERSON PRESS	9
19	ALIBERT, P	MARKETING NOW	SMITHERSON PRESS	15
20	HENDRY, J	COMPUTE-IT	SMITHERSON PRESS	13
21	BAXTER, D	MANAGING CHANGE	SMITHERSON PRESS	12
22	BAXTER, D	SPREADSHEETS FOR MANAGERS	SMITHERSON PRESS	9
23	HENDRY, J	COMPUTING FOR BEGINNERS	SMITHERSON PRESS	12
24	MCDONALD, T	EFFECTIVE OPERATIONS MANAGEMENT	SMITHERSON PRESS	10
25	SMITH, JC	THE MARKETING AGE	SMITHERSON PRESS	7

Database Exercise 10.2 (2)

Record#	AUTHOR	TITLE	PUBLISHER	INSTOCK
1	ALIBERT, P	MARKETING NOW	SMITHERSON PRESS	15
2	ANDREWS, J	EFFECTIVE COMMUNICATIONS	PUTNEY PUBLICATIONS	7
3	BASSEY, S	ADMINISTERING CHANGE	P J THOMSON	16
4	BAXTER, D	MANAGING CHANGE	SMITHERSON PRESS	12
5	BAXTER, D	SPREADSHEETS FOR MANAGERS	SMITHERSON PRESS	9
6	CARRUTHERS, S	ASSERTIVENESS	PUTNEY PUBLICATIONS	15
7	GRAHAM, D	COMPUTERISED STOCK	PUTNEY PUBLICATIONS	10
8	HENDRY, J	COMPUTING FOR BEGINNERS	SMITHERSON PRESS	12
9	HENDRY, J	COMPUTE-IT	SMITHERSON PRESS	13
10	KOSZARY, B	SAFETY AND YOUTH	PUTNEY PUBLICATIONS	15
11	KOSZARY, B	SAFETY NOW	PUTNEY PUBLICATIONS	1
12	MCDONALD, T	EFFECTIVE OPERATIONS MANAGEMENT	SMITHERSON PRESS	10
13	MCQUEEN, K	ALCOHOL AT WORK	PUTNEY PUBLICATIONS	2
14	PASSION, TJ	THE NEW MANAGER	P J THOMSON	5
15	PASSION, TJ	THE MANAGER AND ME	P J THOMSON	15
16	PATTERSON, TD	INTRODUCING COMPUTING	PUTNEY PUBLICATIONS	7
17	PAULS, PT	COMPUTING TODAY	P J THOMSON	2
18	RAE, A	INTRODUCING DATABASE	PUTNEY PUBLICATIONS	10
19	RAE, A	WORD PROCESSING FOR BEGINNERS	PUTNEY PUBLICATIONS	12
20	RAE, A	ADMINISTRATIVE PROCEDURES	SMITHERSON PRESS	9
21	RAE, A	INTRODUCING SPREADSHEETS	PUTNEY PUBLICATIONS	10
22	ROSS, T	MECHANICS FOR TODAY	P J THOMSON	12
23	SMITH, JC	THE MARKETING AGE	SMITHERSON PRESS	7
24	STEEL, S	HAIRDRESSING FOR THE 90'S	SMITHERSON PRESS	2
25	THOMSON, AT	THE COMPUTING AGE	PUTNEY PUBLICATIONS	10

Database Exercise 10.2 (4)

```
Page No.       1
01/01/
                         BOOK LISTING

         Prepared by: Elizabeth A Rae     Dated: Today's Date


BOOK TITLE                      AUTHOR         QUANTITY IN STOCK
----------                      ------         -----------------


** PUBLISHER P J THOMSON
ADMINISTERING CHANGE            BASSEY, S              16
THE NEW MANAGER                 PASSION, TJ             5
THE MANAGER AND ME              PASSION, TJ            15
COMPUTING TODAY                 PAULS, PT               2
MECHANICS FOR TODAY             ROSS, T                12
** Subtotal **
                                                       50


** PUBLISHER PUTNEY PUBLICATIONS
EFFECTIVE COMMUNICATIONS        ANDREWS, J              7
ASSERTIVENESS                   CARRUTHERS,S           15
COMPUTERISED STOCK              GRAHAM, D              10
SAFETY AND YOUTH                KOSZARY, B             15
ALCOHOL AT WORK                 MCQUEEN, K              2
INTRODUCING COMPUTING           PATTERSON,TD            7
INTRODUCING SPREADSHEETS        RAE, A                 10
INTRODUCING DATABASE            RAE, A                 10
WORD PROCESSING FOR BEGINNERS   RAE, A                 12
THE COMPUTING AGE               THOMSON, AT            10
** Subtotal **
                                                       98


** PUBLISHER PUTNEY PUBLICATIONS
SAFETY NOW                      KOSZARY, B              1
** Subtotal **
                                                        1


** PUBLISHER SMITHERSON PRESS
MARKETING NOW                   ALIBERT, P             15
MANAGING CHANGE                 BAXTER, D              12
SPREADSHEETS FOR MANAGERS       BAXTER, D               9
COMPUTE-IT                      HENDRY, J              13
COMPUTING FOR BEGINNERS         HENDRY, J              12
EFFECTIVE OPERATIONS            MCDONALD, T            10
MANAGEMENT
ADMINISTRATIVE PROCEDURES       RAE, A                  9
THE MARKETING AGE               SMITH, JC               7
HAIRDRESSING FOR THE 90'S       STEEL, S                2
** Subtotal **
                                                       89

*** Total ***
                                                      238
```

Database Exercise 11.1

```
Structure for database: A:EX11.1
Number of data records:        20
Date of last update    : 01/01/
Field   Field Name  Type         Width    Dec
    1   TITLE       Character      31
    2   INSTOCK     Numeric         2
    3   AUTHOR      Character      12
    4   MINSTOCK    Numeric         2
** Total **                       48
```

Database Exercise 11.2 (1)

REPORT PRINT OF ALL PUBLICATIONS
WHICH REQUIRE TO BE RE-ORDERED

(RE-ORDER QUANTITIES SHOWN IN NEGATIVE FIGURES)

TITLE OF PUBLICATION	CURRENT STOCK LEVELS	MINIMUM STOCK LEVEL	RE-ORDER QUANTITY
** NAME OF AUTHOR: ALIBERT, P			
MARKETING NOW	15	5	10
** Subtotal **			
	15	5	10
** NAME OF AUTHOR: ANDREWS, J			
EFFECTIVE COMMUNICATIONS	7	10	-3
** Subtotal **			
	7	10	-3
** NAME OF AUTHOR: BASSEY, S			
ADMINISTERING CHANGE	16	5	11
** Subtotal **			
	16	5	11
** NAME OF AUTHOR: BAXTER, D			
MANAGING CHANGE	12	10	2
SPREADSHEETS FOR MANAGERS	9	10	-1
** Subtotal **			
	21	20	1
** NAME OF AUTHOR: CARRUTHERS,S			
ASSERTIVENESS	15	10	5
** Subtotal **			
	15	10	5
** NAME OF AUTHOR: HENDRY, J			
COMPUTE-IT	13	10	3
COMPUTING FOR BEGINNERS	12	10	2
** Subtotal **			
	25	20	5
** NAME OF AUTHOR: KOSZARY, B			
SAFETY NOW	12	9	3
SAFETY AND YOUTH	15	10	5
** Subtotal **			
	27	19	8
** NAME OF AUTHOR: MCDONALD, T			
EFFECTIVE OPERATIONS MANAGEMENT	10	12	-2
** Subtotal **			
	10	12	-2
** NAME OF AUTHOR: PASSION, TJ			
THE NEW MANAGER	5	7	-2

Database Exercise 11.2 (2)

REPORT PRINT OF ALL PUBLICATIONS
WHICH REQUIRE TO BE RE-ORDERED

(RE-ORDER QUANTITIES SHOWN IN NEGATIVE FIGURES)

TITLE OF PUBLICATION	CURRENT STOCK LEVELS	MINIMUM STOCK LEVEL	RE-ORDER QUANTITY
THE MANAGER AND ME	15	9	6
** Subtotal **			
	20	16	4
** NAME OF AUTHOR: PATTERSON,TD			
INTRODUCING COMPUTING	7	10	-3
** Subtotal **			
	7	10	-3
** NAME OF AUTHOR: PAULS, PT			
COMPUTING TODAY	2	5	-3
** Subtotal **			
	2	5	-3
** NAME OF AUTHOR: RAE, A			
INTRODUCING SPREADSHEETS	10	10	0
** Subtotal **			
	10	10	0
** NAME OF AUTHOR: ROSS, T			
MECHANICS FOR TODAY	12	10	2
** Subtotal **			
	12	10	2
** NAME OF AUTHOR: SMITH, JC			
THE MARKETING AGE	7	10	-3
** Subtotal **			
	7	10	-3
** NAME OF AUTHOR: STEEL, S			
HAIRDRESSING FOR THE 90'S	2	5	-3
** Subtotal **			
	2	5	-3
** NAME OF AUTHOR: THOMSON, AT			
THE COMPUTING AGE	10	12	-2
** Subtotal **			
	10	12	-2
*** Total ***			
	206	179	27

Assessment assignment

You are employed in the Personnel Department of a small company and require to carry out a number of tasks in relation to a meeting which will take place 2 weeks from today.

Miss Anderson prefers everything to be in a traditional style, ie displays centred and correctly laid out with font changes and print enhancements used to a maximum.

Task 1

The first task is to send out the Agenda:

AGENDA

Apologies

Minutes of Last Meeting

Matters Arising

Pension Plans

Early Retirements

AOCB

Date of Next Meeting

The secretary of the meeting is J M Scott and the Chairperson is Pamela Anderson, who is also the Personnel Manager.

Task 2

As well as sending out the Agenda, you are also required to send out a covering letter to all committee members inviting them to read over the Minutes and submit any alterations which they see as necessary no later than 5 days from today's date.

You have the facility to complete this task by entering the details into a mailing list in your Database program and then merging with the relevant letter. You will find the names and home addresses on the attached sheet headed MEMBERS' HOME ADDRESSES AND TELEPHONE NUMBERS.

Task 3

Pamela is also keen that you enclose a copy of the holiday entitlement for each employee and you should mention this in the letter. You are required to calculate this by using your Spreadsheet program, but she would prefer that it be printed out using either your word processing program or DTP in order that you may embolden headings, etc.

Employee's Name	Annual Holidays	J	F	M	A	M	J	J	A	S	Total	Bal
Andrews, J C	25		2	5		14						
Cuthberts, A	25			3		21						
Costa, A J	30	2.5			7.5				21			
Duncan, P	25	2			3				14			
Forbes, L	30	2.5				10			0.5	5		
Haston, J C	21	2		1		2		14				
Jones, J F	25		1.5			7.5			10			
Lyons, W	21		2		10				7			
Mason, C	25		3			7			7			
Mathews, M	21	2			7			10				

Use the instructions given on the attached sheet for calculating holiday entitlement.

Once this file has been imported within a WP or DTP program, insert a note after the table to say that this is from Jan–Sept only and an update will be issued shortly prior to printing a copy for reference purposes.

Task 4

The Minutes of the last meeting are as follows:

MINUTES of Meeting held in The Sports Club on Friday, 23 March 19—.

PRESENT:	P Anderson (Chairperson) J M Scott (Secretary) J Rice (Treasurer) P Patterson J Jamieson
APOLOGIES:	Mr Baxter sent his apologies via Mr Jamieson
MINUTES:	The Minutes of the previous meeting, which had been distributed earlier, were accepted by the meeting and signed by the Chairperson.
MATTERS ARISING:	Mr Rice raised the question of holiday entitlement of employees with more than 5 years' service. Miss Anderson assured him that records of all holidays taken and subsequently due to be taken were retained and it was agreed to submit copies to all members prior to the next meeting.
SPORTS CLUB MEMBERSHIP:	Membership fees for the Sports Club were discussed and the following agreed: Single Membership: £25.00 per annum Family Membership: £75.00 per annum (2 adults/2 children)
CHEESE & WINE:	It was agreed that the social event, ie the Cheese & Wine party, would be held on the first Friday in August (insert the date here) in the Sports Club at 7.30 pm for 8.00 pm.
AOCB:	No further business was raised.
NEXT MEETING:	The next meeting will be held on (insert relevant date according to Agenda) at 7.30 pm.

Task 5

Using your DTP program, put together a notice informing staff of the Cheese & Wine night, including an appropriate caption to make it more effective.

Task 6

You notice from your files that the following holidays have been taken – this is after you have completed the spreadsheet task – and you require to retrieve your file and recalculate as follows:
   Up to December the following applies:

J C Andrews had 2 days off in October and 1 day in November
A Cuthberts had 1 day off in November
P Duncan had 2 days off in November
L Forbes had 5 days off in November
J F Jones had 1 day off in October and 2 in November
C Mason had 7 days off in November and 1 day in December

1 Make the additional calculations, editing the formulae as necessary

2 Insert an appropriate heading at the beginning of your worksheet

3 Using an appropriate formula, calculate an additional column which shows any employee with more than 5 days' holiday still to take

4 A further 3 staff members who joined in October require to be added. They have an entitlement of 6 days each:
   J Smith
   P Thomson
   A Rae

5 J Smith had 2 days off in November

6 Take a further printout in your spreadsheet program of columns which contain Employees' Names, Total Used, Balance, and a column which demonstrates who has more than 5 days to take

7 Produce a graph detailing cumulative holidays taken each quarter, ie total holidays taken from January-March, April-June, July-September, October-December

8 Give the graph a suitable title, saving it for importing at a later stage

9 Now load this spreadsheet file to WP or DTP in order to display it more effectively and insert an appropriate paragraph as per task 3

Task 7

You have finished the work in relation to the meeting and are now required to enter the following information into a database file:

Employee's Name	Date of Birth	Start Date	Finish Date	Retirement Date	Sickness	Weekly Pay
Andrews, J C	03.09.56	04.07.74			12	223.00
Cuthberts, A	04.10.55	07.10.77			5	200.00
Costa, A J	05.11.52	12.12.80			10	225.00
Cunningham, C	12.03.68	10.03.85	21.05.86		14	
Duncan, P	06.07.49	12.06.82			7	279.00
Donaldson, A	07.06.50	17.07.83	21.07.89		0	
Forbes, L	07.06.44	18.06.60			4	250.00
Haston, J C	21.12.46	19.12.70			12	200.00
Jones, J F	28.11.40	28.11.56			5	225.00
Lyons, W	21.10.30	12.01.50			7	275.00
Mason, C	22.11.30	12.01.50			5	315.75
Matthews, M	21.02.31	12.01.50			14	275.75
Smith, J	22.07.60	22.10.91			0	150.00
Thomson, P	12.12.56	22.10.91			0	150.00
Rae, A	02.03.66	22.10.91			1	150.00

1 Your database fields should be appropriately selected and relevant field sizes entered

2 You are required to calculate, using your database program, the retirement date of all employees

Printouts required:

1 Listing of all employee details (ie full file)

2 Report format for all employees sorted into alphabetical order

3 Employees with earnings less than or equal to £150.00 per week

4 Index by Employee Name

5 Index by Date of Birth

6 Index by Weekly Pay

7 Listing of all employees with less than 5 years to go until retirement

8 Listing of all employees with more than 35 years' service and earning less than £300.00 per week

9 Amend all records meeting the criteria in (8) to earnings of £300 per week

Task 8

On completion of task 7, you should transfer the file contents to either your WP or DTP program and display it more effectively, taking a printout of the entire file – excluding sickness days – and highlighting the employees with less than 5 years to retirement.
    Before you do this, please delete all employees who are no longer with the company.

Task 9

Key the following information into a macro file, printing out one copy on completion:

MEMORANDUM

TO: See distribution   FROM: Personnel

SUBJECT: Holiday trend   DATE:

The following graph shows the holiday trend for this year:

This should help with departmental planning in the next financial year.

Distribution:

Task 10

Retrieve the graph prepared earlier and import it into the memorandum prepared in task 9. The distribution list is as follows:

Costing
Production
Stores
Distribution

PERSONNEL DEPARTMENT

Instructions for calculating holiday entitlement using a spreadsheet program:

1 Set the global column width to 7

2 Set local column widths as required

3 Right-justify the headings

4 Set the global format as fixed with 1 decimal place

5 Set the range containing annual holidays as fixed with 0 decimal places

6 Calculate the total holidays used by each employee

7 Calculate the balance due to each employee

8 Calculate the holidays taken each month by all employees

9 Print out the data from your spreadsheet program prior to transfer to DTP/WP

10 Save your file as HOLIDAY

11 Save only the headings and employee names in a master file in order that it may be used in a subsequent year

PERSONNEL DEPARTMENT

MEMBERS' HOME ADDRESSES AND TELEPHONE NUMBERS

Mr J M Scott
13 Anderson Drive
MOTHERWELL
ML10 2TZ

(0698) 87990

Mr Jonathan Rice
22 North St
MOTHERWELL
ML10 2TZ

(0698) 20390

Mr James Baxter
19 High Circular Road
MOTHERWELL
ML10 9JJ

(0698) 28990

Miss Pauline Patterson
22 High Station Road
FALKIRK
FK1 7HQ

(0324) 27611

Mr James Jamieson
19 Park Crescent
FALKIRK
FK8 0JJ

(0786) 67891